The No Close, Close

Skyrocket Your Sales With The Ultimate Three Step "Sell Without Selling" Formula

3 Steps:

Position, Persuade, Get Paid!

MARK TOSONI

Edited & Designed by Ken Christensen
Rally Cat Media
321-409-1260
www.RallyCatMedia.com

Published by Game Changer Publishing
www.PublishaBestSellingBook.com

Printed in the United States of America.

DEDICATION

I would like to dedicate this book to the bravest souls in the business world: ***Commissioned Sales Professionals***.

Anyone who has walked this path knows the mental toughness required to deal with the jungle we navigate daily. Yet, with the correct skill and mindset - along with the correct deployment strategy - Success Is Inevitable.

I'm ecstatic that God has called me to Inspire, Educate, Impact and Motivate Commission Sales Professionals to reach their Highest Potential, and I've been doing just that since I heard the call way back in a seminar room in 1994. I am one of you, I admire you and I am here to serve you at the highest level that I can find within my being.

Sincerely,
Mark Tosoni

ACKNOWLEDGMENTS

I would like to acknowledge my amazing wife, Aurora. I'm only half the size without you. You inspire me, push me, and keep me in the game when I want to give up. Somehow, you keep me going strong. This one is for you – the greatest wife and mother a man could ever ask for.

Also, thank you to Ken Christensen for all your creative help and to all the sales people I work with and have worked with along the way. I love solving our problems. Thank you for demonstrating courage; it's humbling, to say the least.

And, of course, to all my kids and the *"Dream Team,"* Mark and Micah, for stretching me to find my greatness, thank you. We're pulling this off, my little guys!

Table of Contents

Foreword

by Ben Gay III

I have been in this game for 40 years and having worked with the likes of Zig Ziglar, Napoleon Hill, Og Mandino and the best sales people on planet earth. I AM the author of "The Closers" sales book series and my books have sold over 10 million copies.

Every now and then a Really Great Book and Really Great Sales Talent comes forth and I believe this book "The No Close Close" offers game changing concepts and that's coming from me, a guy who's made a life of selling and teaching people how to close sales and double and triple their incomes.

The fundamentals of the sales game are the same today as they were years ago yet the customers access to information calls for a slightly different approach because they have so many options at their fingertips and Marks book addresses these distinctions.

Ironically this guy has been a student of mine since the early 90's. He was a struggling salesman with dreams of wealth and success. He would literally run alarm appointments daily at 11, 3 and 7pm, come home and study The Closers and work out the closes that he missed during the day with The Closers books as his guide. This went on for several years and finally success began to fall in his lap. He went on to become one the best Alarm Sales People in the Country.

Soon thereafter he began building alarm sales teams and replicated his success selling 10's and 10's and 10's of thousands of Alarm Systems. He went on to literally write the book on alarm sales titled "Alarm Sales Mastery".

In 2017 he shifted gears and took his skillset into the solar industry and along with his partners built his companies sales to over 2 million dollars a week in less than 24 months. That's what happens when you become a Master Closer, you can rinse and repeat your success over and over again. You can go sell at a massively high level yourself, you can teach others, or both. Mark has proven this beyond a doubt.

I was so impressed with his story, his success and his Three Step Formula that has become the ultimate sell without selling formula, that I invited him to be a distinguished co-author of the Closers series. We will be co-writing a closers book together titled Master "The Closers" Mindset ....Crack The Code That Will Double, Even Triple, Your Income In The Sales Game!

Mark is a dynamic guy who is not only a mega successful salesman but leader, entrepreneur, family man and mentor to thousands of commission sales people that he's taught this craft to. He is a very successful real estate investor as well and the creator of the "Magnetize Your Millions "Podcast with his oldest daughter Lindsey Torres.

The author of eleven books, all his books and programs are designed to empower and uplift the sales professionals and I'm now honored to call him a friend!

If you have the privilege to train with Mark I highly recommend it, your skill level, mindset and confidence will soar. Inevitably, you make more money... Lots and Lots More Money!

~ Ben Gay III, Author of "The Closers"

Why I Am In Sales?

As a Sales Professional I am a
High Level Problem Solver!

The Purpose Of My Career…

To earn money in excess of my expenses by miles.
So that I can invest that into residual income streams.
So that my residual income can exceed my expenses.
Once this is accomplished its Game Over!

Rinse and repeat if you choose!

Introduction

It was the fall of 1985 when I was sitting in a college lecture, staring at the walls thinking "how am I going to make money?" As the year continued, my urge to generate income grew and grew and I found myself thinking about how I was going to make more money than my college professors are. The only problem was, I didn't know how. At the end of the second semester, I decided to give my father the bad news; I wasn't going to return to college. I still didn't know what I was going to do. I just knew that I wanted to make money and college wasn't my path.

Several years earlier, I had met the boyfriend of a co-worker named Sharon who happened to sell cars. During that summer after college, we reconnected. And by September, I was officially selling cars. My father was upset because he had his Ph.D. and had dreams and aspirations of a formally educated son. He was very let down, but I stayed true to myself and just knew my path was different. So, my car sales career began, but it was crystal clear that I knew nothing about selling cars. How could I quickly change that?

The next steps seemed so natural. I turned to books, cassette tape programs, and seminars. I can remember the very first book I read was Unlimited Power by Tony Robbins and the very first cassette program I listened to was by Tom Hopkins, How to Master the Art of Selling. I was so inspired by these programs that something woke up inside of me; a dream began to emerge with the excitement of possibility. In a peer group of employees, I began to open my mind to what was possible.

The owner of the car dealership wore a Rolex. At the time, to me, Rolex equaled success. The sales manager was making six figures, the used car sales manager was making six figures and the finance & insurance (F&I) manager was making six figures. I started to believe that I also could make six figures and that is when I developed my dream of becoming a millionaire. I really had no evidence to prove that I could pull this off. Yet, being in this environment convinced me that if I was willing to work for it and I learned how to sell, I could achieve my dream. So, I went for it!

Now, I actually did pretty well for a guy with no sales experience and no real-life experience. I was making decent money at the car dealership, but I was still struggling because it was a 100% straight commission; you eat what you kill. This went on for the next four years and then I began to grow restless. I felt like I could make more money in direct sales or outside sales and so I started to look around and decided that I was going to sell insurance.

This is where I bit off a little more than I could chew because with insurance, it was basically door-to-door and cold calling by phone. At that time, I didn't know it, but I had a very serious fear of rejection. It was a little different when people were coming into a car dealership looking for a car versus going out to them and soliciting them to buy something. It was a whole different skill set. As I look back at this time, although it was difficult and I was starving, barely able to put groceries on the table for my new young wife and little girl, I was following that dream.

I didn't get much support from the people around me, nor did they see what I saw that I could make something with my life and I was really hungry to do it. Sure, I was working on the mindset and I didn't have the skillset, but I did have a burning desire. My insurance career went on for two years and I was becoming more and more desperate. In fact, I got so desperate that I actually contemplated doing something illegal to keep my head above water and to pay the bills. Thank God I didn't! I was begging the universe for support. I had read the books, I had listened to the tapes, but there was something more that I needed. I didn't know what it was, I just knew I needed help.

Then, by a strange act of fate, a mentor entered my life and everything rapidly changed, but not without struggle. My mentor's name was Mike, and he was the kid brother of my father's best friend. Mike was very successful in sales in his early 20s. He never went to college and I'm guessing that Mike didn't get named "Most Likely To Succeed" in high school. But Mike is one of the most competitive people that I've ever met to this day. His way of being and way of thinking was about to rub off on me in ways that would eventually turn me into a millionaire. One day I was visiting Mike, and he showed me how to close sales, how to keep a positive attitude and how to do demos. Mike had all the answers to all my questions.

I excitedly walked into Mike's office and he said to me,

"See that little box over there?" I said, "Yes!"

He continued, "I just sold three of them."

I said, "Really? What are they?"

Mike said, "They are Alarm Systems." "How would you like to join me in a new venture? I want to start a company selling alarms."

Now to this point, I could see myself maybe someday becoming a sales manager. Never in a million years did I think I would wind up owning my own business. It just wasn't a realistic goal in my mind. And yet, when Mike propositioned me and without any thought (take note of this), I said.

"Yes."

I had found a mentor in an industry I would soon grow to love.

Mike took me on the road with him and I watched him sell 25 security systems in a row without missing a single sale. Granted, some of those sales were canceled, but Mike built my belief system like a Mack truck. The time came for me to get on the road and start selling myself, but it didn't come so easy to me. I went through 11 demonstrations and didn't get a single sale. I was discouraged and I didn't know what I was going to do. I had a young family, my back was against the wall and I needed to make money. So, on that Saturday morning of my 12th demo, I made a new decision, and that decision was this,

"I'm not leaving this house without a sale!"

Something happens when we make what I like to call *"Real Decisions."* When we amplify our decisions to the level where they become, *"Succeed Or Die!"*

Success was my only option. I went to that house that morning and did the demo of my life, and on my 12th attempt, I walked out with a sale. I could literally hear the Rocky theme playing in my head. I now knew if I could just replicate what I did over and over again, I would be successful!

Six months passed and I did OK, not great, but I was making some sales. Still, Mike was not satisfied with my performance. He called me into the office one day and said,

> *"Hey, you got a minute?"*

> *"Listen, you're not getting it done, so I'm going to give you two choices and I want an answer by tomorrow morning. Choice Number One, you can exit the business altogether or choice Number Two, you could take a reduction in pay. And again you can let me know by tomorrow what you're going to do."*

It was harsh. It was brash and let's just say it was a really good shot to the head and I was teed off. Fortunately for me, I have been a hockey player since I was a young boy and one thing I knew how to do was fight. When I got home that night, I went into my basement and proceeded to beat up my heavy bag and my karate bag to get out the frustration. I was really upset. I called a few friends and of course, my friends told me, *"Screw Mike, you don't need him! He's selfish! Get out of there."*

That night I reflected on it and decided that I wasn't going to follow their advice. I was going to stay but take less money. I went in the next day and told my mentor Mike, *"I'm staying!"*

Again, something major shifted. I didn't just say I was staying with fire inside, I said,

> *"I'm staying and I'm going to shove my success so far up your rear end that you'll never know what hit you."*

I was fighting mad! Mike was a master of motivation and knew I needed a fight, so he cared enough to give me one.

It was years earlier, while I was playing high school hockey that I made varsity at a Massachusetts hockey power and I sat on the bench for most of the year. I had never sat out before. The coach didn't tell me why nor did he pay any attention to me at all. I had always been a standout hockey player and I didn't understand what was happening. As the year went on, I grew angrier and angrier. And with a week left of the season, I just didn't show up; I quit the team. Mike knew this and he used this against me to get under my skin in a way nobody ever had.

That said, the next year I went to a rival hockey power. In my mind, I didn't see this as quitting. I saw this as changing my approach and I was very happy at the new school. This school was where I wanted to go from the beginning, but my father had sort of forced me to go to a private Catholic school and I always hated it. As it so happened, in my junior year, we wound up in the Western Massachusetts' championship against the team that sat me out. And like what I've said earlier about real decisions, I made a real decision that night to, "Succeed or die." That was my game, and I was willing to die for it.

By the time the final buzzer sounded, the score was 5 - 4 and I had scored a goal and added an assist. My presence was a major catalyst in winning that game. I do remember skating by the bench, not saying a word, looking at my old coach and the team I played for the year before in the greatest sports victory of my high school career. Little did I realize during this time that I formed a belief. Beliefs can be very powerful in holding us back from success. The belief I had previously formed was,

> *"If I give it my all, I'm only going to be let down. So, I'm not going to give my all."*

That changed that day of the game. I used my anger to get revenge and that is a very good short time strategy. But it's not a long-term strategy.

Fast forward to when I'm selling Alarm Systems and my mentor Mike knew somehow that I wasn't giving my all and he challenged me in a way that was deeper than anyone had ever challenged me. Today I call this a *"Defining Moment"* and I am forever grateful to Mike for pushing me to my highest potential at that moment. When he challenged me, I vowed that no one would ever question my value again. I would bring so much to the table, to the customer, to the business, to the training, and to my partners that I would overwhelm people with effectiveness and that's exactly what I set out to do. I poured myself into new books, new tapes, and new seminars. In fact, I carried around a micro-cassette recorder and hung on every word Mike said for four years and I copied all his best practices. This is called modeling.

Little did I realize at the time that this was a Serious Success Strategy. Within a year's time, my income had grown to more than six figures, and within three years, I did my first financial statement as I was buying my first investment property. I looked down at the financial statement and realized that I was a millionaire, and I was only 28 years old! It was a dream come true. Unfortunately, this success only lasted for a year and then I sabotaged myself. On some unconscious level, I was uncomfortable with this success and found a way to make it disappear. I would walk my dog out on the green belt near my home, smoking cigarettes because I would tend to hurt myself when my life wasn't working out the way I wanted. We will talk more about this throughout the book.

So there, I was smoking and asking God what happened. How did I go from being a broke struggling salesman to a millionaire in my twenties and how did I lose that? How could I prevent this from ever happening again? How do I get it back and then some? These questions became an obsession for me, and the rest of this book will answer these questions. I will take you on a journey through my story step by step on how I was able to turn this around, not only to become a millionaire but a multi-millionaire, and how I've been able to turn that into permanent wealth.

So, welcome to *The No Close, Close*. You're about to learn the ultimate three-step system to skyrocket yourself beyond your wildest dreams which you will soon realize is the foundation for most wealthy people's success. *Let's get started!*

CHAPTER 1

The Mindset of a Commission Sales Millionaire

"It is your mindset that puts your skill set on steroids!"

~ Mark Tosoni

Notes & Ideas

CHAPTER 1

The Mindset of a Commission Sales Millionaire

Any time we're going to talk about mindset or how your mind is set it's going to lead into a conversation about the power of belief.

So, what is belief? Tony Robbins says beliefs are thoughts we are certain are real. They are references or experiences we've had that we come to believe are true.

There is a story of a farmer who lived way out in the country. One day he was visited by a guest, they were having such a great time and it got late so he invited his guest to stay in the guest house. He walked him over and got him all set up in his guest house and they all went to bed. Sometime in the middle of the night the guest got up to go to the bathroom. When he went into the bathroom in his sleepy state he thought he saw a huge coiled up snake.

In the morning, the farmer got up and was knocking on the door to invite his guest to a home cooked breakfast. There was no answer. He continued to knock with no answer, and he thought this was strange, he thought something was wrong. So, he got his key, and he went in. As he entered the guest house he was shocked to see his friend on the floor. He checked his pulse, and he was dead. He was lying on the ground right next to a huge coiled up hose. He didn't die from a snake bite, he died from what he believed was a snake; he died from fear!

This story depicts the *Power Of Belief.* Belief will give you life, but it can also give you death. Belief can give you struggle, or belief can give you ease. In the following pages you are going to learn how to use belief to give you ease.

YOUR DOMINANT PATTERN OF ENERGY

Many years ago, I coined the acronym DPOE. It stands for *Your Dominant Pattern Of Energy.* Your beliefs or things you've come to know as true from your experience literally form an energy field around you, this energy field becomes your dominant pattern of energy. The interesting thing is when it comes to belief, it is self-validating. In other words, when you have a belief unconsciously you will do everything you can to validate that belief regardless of whether that leads you to struggle or ease; it's what humans do with belief.

The quality of your doing is being filtered through your beliefs. Everything you do is being filtered through what you believe. The way you speak, the way you walk, the volume at which you speak, the speed at which you speak, how you look at people, the words you use. Everything is being filtered through your belief system. Interestingly enough the people you speak to are also filtering you through their belief system. This becomes an interesting dynamic in a sales situation and a call for you, the *Sales Professional,* to *Master The Game Of Belief* and when you do, your life and sales career will get really fun.

First you must learn to master your own beliefs; how to let old ones go and how to create new ones. Once you learn this, you can learn how to change the beliefs of others. Here is where you become very powerful as a person of influence.

In the Bible, The book of Mathew 9:29 it states,

> *"It is done unto you as you believe."*

These words I have come to learn through years of experience are very true. The challenge some people have is they don't see themselves as the cause of what is happening in their life; they see themselves at the effect. Meaning they see themselves as being victimized by our universe or its inhabitants. The belief of whether you are the cause or whether you are the effect is your choice. However, I will tell you this; having worked with salespeople, thousands of them for decades, I have learned that the ones who believe they are the cause of their circumstance are the ones that make the most money. So, I invite you right here, right now, to begin to believe that YOU are the cause of your circumstances and start to believe in the power of belief, your own belief. It has blown me away how things have mysteriously showed up in my life as I've continued to level up my belief it has become undeniable.

The interesting thing about belief is belief also makes up something we call identity and identity is essentially how we see ourselves; it is made up of what we believe we are and who we believe we are.

In the Bible, The Book of Mark 12:31 a clue is left,

> *"Love Your Neighbor As Yourself."*

It is teaching us to love and value ourselves because our lives come forth from this. Your identity actually precedes belief. Here's a little million-dollar secret: if you want to really create rapid change in your business, start to shift your identity. Once you begin to shift how you see yourself, beliefs actually become even more pliable and easy to change. You will always get feedback from the universe, from your matrix, reflecting exactly what it is you believe if you are willing to take a look.

BAR: Belief... Action... Results!

Once you begin to shift your identity and you begin to shift your beliefs it is very easy to raise the BAR. You do this by leveling up the way you see yourself and you do this by leveling up the way you believe. When you do, your actions reflect this new identity and your actions reflect your new beliefs because the results must match. I've heard several people say throughout my career,

> *"You don't get what you want, you get who you are,"*

and this is exactly what they're talking about. You get who you are in life. You get how you see yourself and you get what you believe about yourself; this is what you get in life. Do you want more? Simply shift the way you see yourself and shift what you believe in, brace yourself it's about to get real.

Let's look at some examples:

"I believe people aren't safe" or "I don't trust people" vs. "people are here to support me in my dreams". "People love to support me in sales, total strangers even support me, everywhere I go I'm supported, I'm always in the right place

at the right time". Which set of beliefs do you think will serve you better in sales?

How many of you would like to raise the bar? Then just say *"Yes!*

The Three Myths:

I'm not worthy
I'm not good enough
I don't deserve.

So many of us were not taught that we are worth something. Many of us were put down, many of us feel undeserving. You will know this is you if you are struggling in sales. Granted, maybe you're new and so you're learning a new skill set and you struggle because of it. But make no mistake about it, what is really driving the bus is what's underneath; these unconscious beliefs that will wreak havoc on your career if left unchecked.

Here's some really cool ideas that come from scripture to validate what we're talking about here.

In Genesis 1:27 it says,

> *"We are created in the image and likeness of God."*

But before that in Genesis 1 it says,

> *"In the beginning God CREATED the heavens and the earth."*

So, the first thing God says about Himself is that He is *"A Creator."* We are created in His image and likeness therefore you are a creator, not The Creator, but a creator.

Let that sink in. If this doesn't begin to shift your identity, nothing will. Believe these words will change your game at levels you cannot even see. This truly changes everything. Meditate on this, let this dominate your consciousness that you are a creator. You are not the effect of the things you want, you are the cause, depending on the level that you allow this truth into your life.

Let's talk about money. In The Book of Genesis 3 God says,

"Gold is good."

Our monetary system is a modern-day version of what once was based on gold. Hopefully, as of this writing, our monetary system will be back to the gold standard that it used to be, but that's another story. In this book I'm working on your belief system. Some of us have a lot of unsupportive beliefs about money. My belief aligns with Genesis 3 Where God says, *"Gold is good."* I would invite you to adopt this mentality, especially if you're going to stay in commission sales. If you believe something is wrong with money or that something is wrong with people with money why would you want to create and generate that in your life? Choose beliefs that will support you, let go of beliefs that do not.

Beliefs are first developed in us at an early age. Most people don't realize that we have the power to choose new beliefs. Belief is nothing but a choice. What type of choices would you now like to make for your life?

By far one of my favorite Bible verses states,

"Be transformed by the renewing of your mind." - Romans 2:12

This speaks to changing belief and that it is your job to transform and to renew your mind.

THE DIFFERENCE BETWEEN A CLOSER AND A CROOK

Some salespeople believe sales is doing something to people, in truth it's something you do for them. If you're in it to win it for the long haul, begin to think about people long term. Begin to get obsessed with solving your clients' problem issues and pain. Take the time to discover what drives them, what's important to them and how the pain of their issue is affecting them. Sales really comes down to intent, and the difference between a closer and a crook is merely intention. The crook intends to do something to someone, the closer does something for them. *Get It, Got It, Good!*

Are you ready for some millionaire beliefs?

WHAT MILLIONAIRES BELIEVE

"Success requires diligence". Most people describe this as hard work. I work a lot and I work often, by choice, but it's not hard. The hard part is optional and is usually based on internal resistance. That said, be prepared to be diligent because success requires it. You must do the work if you choose success.

"I persist relentlessly". To be a millionaire requires grit, you must be persistent and prepared to be relentless to overcome obstacles both seen and unseen.

"I change my approach but never give up". Success requires major flexibility. Quitting is not an option once you dedicate your life to mastery. Changing your approach is mandatory.

Always pay attention and reflect on feedback and change and adjust wherever necessary.

"Wealth takes place over a lifetime". I once heard Tony Robbins say:

> *"Change takes place in an instant."*

I know this is true or can be true, yet it also takes place over time. Think long term because it's a long-term game.

Millionaires know they are creators. Creators don't give their power away to resentment, anger, excuses or blame. It is clear that God states He's a creator in the book of Genesis. He later says we are created in His likeness and image. Bottom line, we are creators and as a creator what are you going to create? You can not be a creator and play the role of victim at the same time.

All the top-level performers I know believe in a higher power; they might not agree on what it is but they all have a relationship with it . There comes a point in success where you will think,

> *"Wow, I'm good, but something else is at work here."*

That's the higher power I choose to call God.

"I Love People, I Love Myself".* "The universe is a mirror", *"self-love and love of others is the ultimate influence".

"I'm Worthy By Virtue Of My Birth". Your identity is the foundation of all results. From it your beliefs come forth, and your actions and results follow. Leveling up your value and worthiness are guaranteed to get your cash register ringing.

"I Am Enough". This is a tricky one for many people because we are taught we are not enough. It's a lie, a big and damaging one. Begin to know you are enough by virtue of your birth on this planet.

I Deserve The Best Of Everything

"I am God like; I create". I am God like and I create therefore I am a force that is causative. I am not at the effect of life; I am the cause. In our culture we've been taught to play the role of the victim, that life is happening to us versus happening for us and through us. We are causing it vibrationally. More on that later.

"Gold is money, money is good". We get what we focus on. Eventually it winds up in our reticular activating system in our brain. Once this happens, we search for evidence to make it true. By focusing on money as good, you will bring evidence to your life that this is true.

"I serve people", "I use money", "people before profit", "profit next". There is a law in the universe called the Law Of Life and it basically states that the universe always favors more life. So, when you serve people, you are aligning with this law. When you use people, you are out of alignment with this law; flow with the river, not against it.

"I always generate way more than my expenses by miles". The number one habit to enhance your sales career is to always make more money than your expenses. I've observed salespeople try to take on side hustles before they get this

correct. This is a mistake! If you follow my philosophy, beliefs are a practice, I practice believing. Choose any one belief and focus on it for a period of 30 days. You can read it in a book or say it out loud. It will start to take root in your mind. You get what you focus on. Where is your focus?

Here are a few power beliefs I would invite you to start to work on...

- ***Money Is A Spiritual Substance Turned Physical.*** I am here to steward it. Energy can neither be created nor destroyed. Money is essentially the energy of exchange. If you steward it correctly, it will work for you. If you do not, in true energy fashion, it will move somewhere that will.

- ***Money Comes To Me Like A Magnet.*** Believe it and it will be. Enough said.

- ***I Love To Grow My Money***. Money is not meant to be stagnant; it must be used strategically. Spend some on your expenses, give some to something that inspires you, save some and pay yourself first, invest some in something that will generate cash flow, pay as little in taxes as legally possible and have fun in the process.

- ***Money Works For Me.*** Does your money work for you, or do you work for it? It will work for you if you believe it works for you, but you must do the correct things with it.

- ***I Am Masterful With Money.*** Start to tell yourself you are masterful with money and tell a new story around it.

- ***I Am The Cause Of All That Happens In My Life.*** You truly are a causative creator. Notice this is one of the biggest breakthrough beliefs for you to become wealthy.

- ***I Am The Controller Of My Vibration***. The one thing that people can control in their life. Most go into the act of victimhood instead of managing what they're thinking and feeling. Focus on this. It takes a little work, but anyone can do this.

- ***I Am A Wealth Magnet.*** Yes, you are. Believe it. See yourself this way and it will begin to happen for you. You get what you focus on most of the time.

My question is this, if you were to believe all of the beliefs that I just stated, do you think you will change your results? Who do you think you would become? In order to internalize these beliefs, you must see them, hear them and feel them daily for them to take root in your mind; you get what you focus on.

Action Step

Your Action Step is to copy these and put them somewhere where you can review them daily until they take root in your mind. You must be persistent with this; how much do you desire the next level of your life? Your hunger determines your destiny.

CHAPTER 2

Purpose Pays, Fear Weighs

"He who has a Why to live for can bear any How!"
~ Frederick Nietzsche

Notes & Ideas

CHAPTER 2

Purpose Pays, Fear Weighs

Having been in the sales game since age 20, when I look back it's really easy to see patterns. As of this writing I am now 53 years young so when I look back I can clearly see where I made choices out of fear versus knowingness. Much of this was due to the fact that I wasn't really clear on the purpose of my career. Clarity has tremendous power. In a moment, you are going to gain tremendous clarity, a new clarity, the clarity you likely have not been operating with. As a result, you will no longer be susceptible to making career decisions that do not serve you.

By my 31st birthday, I had sold a company I had built after the company that I sabotaged. I went back into business six months after I sabotaged my first company that I spoke about in the introduction and re-built another company and then five years into it I sold it to my partner. At the end of the buyout which lasted two years I was getting anxious because I didn't know what I was going to do. So, I sought the guidance of my mentor, Mike, who had now moved out of state and was running a window company in North Carolina. So, Mike was starting to sell this "Lifetime Paint Job Product." So, I left Florida that summer and traveled to Charlotte, North Carolina and began to learn how to sell this exterior paint product.

Leads were coming in through the newspaper and Mike was doing about $400,000.00 a month in sales. I knew if I took this product back to Orlando, Florida, I could build a sales team throughout the state and build a really big business. On the outside things looked really good, but on the inside I was really fearful. My buyout was coming to an end and I couldn't get back into the alarm business because of the buyout and I didn't know what I was going to do next. So clearly I was living in fear.

At the end of the summer I returned to Orlando, Florida. It was now September 2001. 9-11 happened. I had just set my office up and running and suddenly, everything stopped. After 9-11, we could no longer get leads. People were not responding and by December, I had closed the business down losing about $40,000.00 Take note, I was learning how to follow my *Inner Guidance System.*

Had I been clearer on my purpose for my sales career I might've been able to avoid the stress, the anxiety and the monetary loss from this experience. So let me get down to it, the purpose of your sales career is this,

> *"To generate more money than your expenses by miles so that you can use the excess for investment purposes and so your residual income can exceed your expenses, so that you become free."*

Once you complete that, it's game over. Rinse and repeat if you choose. Had I been clear on this I probably would've never sold my Alarm Systems company to begin with. I wound up back in the alarm business.

So, it's important to be aware of how you are making decisions and choices in your career. Simply ask yourself,

> *"Where am I coming from and how does this make me feel?"*

Take the time to tune in. Heavy and confusing equals fear, light and clear equals Love.

Fear will weigh you down. I could write a whole book about my life experiences, how I came from fear and how things didn't work out. Remember this, fear contracts and love expands, so if your career or sales or money are contracting you can always trace that back to fear. If your career or sales or money are expanding that is because you are coming from a place of purpose and passion and love. The idea here is for you to find your unique path that you love so that you will expand.

TANGIBLE PRODUCTS VERSUS INTANGIBLE

Now this is a very interesting concept that also took me years to become aware of. This could end up saving you lots and lots of time so that you can get focused on the purpose of your sales career. I was doing pretty well in car sales. I was paying my expenses, I was young, but I was making $35 - $40,000 a year. This is in the late 80s, not bad for a 22 year-old but as time went on I became restless in car sales because I saw a vision for my life. I wanted to be a six-figure earner and I eventually wanted to become a millionaire.

Unlike the car sales job that was totally presented to me by my friend Joe, (please take note of that part where it was presented to me), I now took my fate into my own hands and went out looking for a job. I had this dream I wanted to make six figures and I wanted to become a millionaire. I found myself in the insurance sales business.

I was very ballsy at this age considering I had a wife and a young child at home. I was following a dream and I was not going to be denied. However, I was not very wise, nor did I have very good guidance. The next two years of my sales career were a disaster and it wasn't just because I was out door knocking and cold calling over the telephone, the truth is even when I had a referral or a company lead I just wasn't very good at selling insurance, and I really wasn't good on the cold call. The reality is, some salespeople are, and some aren't. It's based on certain instincts that are built into you as a human being and of course this can be profiled today and easily determined. Had I profiled myself I would have never taken that sales position.

I'll make a long story short; I was literally having to call family members to bring over groceries, I was that broke. I was contemplating doing something illegal. I was seriously contemplating this. I needed money badly but by God's grace I didn't do it. I know this road of straight commission can be challenging because it's all I've ever known, But I also know there's massive upside if you can clarify some of these key points.

When I look back at my experiences in the Alarm Systems business and car sales as well as the solar sales and installation company I own now, I've discovered that I excel with tangible products more so then I did with an intangible product. Now it could come down to my passion for the product or maybe it came down to being able to see tangible results with a tangible product. Do you think I gravitate more towards a tangible product or intangible product? A product or service?

Take note, because this might turn out to play a role in you finding your unique path. I know it did for me. It's not only a matter of whether or not the product is tangible or intangible. There is another piece to it. A really big piece to this puzzle for me is whether or not you are involved in a product or a process that you absolutely love and can get very passionate about.

In Chapter Three you are going to learn something called a *Healthy View Of Selling*. I will just tell you that one part of that definition is that you are expressing yourself through a product that you love. If you are not expressing yourself through a product or service that you love whether intangible or tangible you are limiting your ability to generate income in excess of your expenses to a large enough degree where you would be able to move into investing for cash flow. So this whole piece about finding the right product for you, tangible versus intangible, something you love versus something maybe you only like, this is a small hinge that is going to swing a massive door.

FIND YOUR CRUSADE, YOUR FIELD OF FAVOR

It was December 1991 when my mentor Mike and I got into the Alarm Systems business. I thought it would be a great business because it had the ability to generate residual income and my mind was on residual income at that time. Not to mention that we could make a lot of money along the way. Clearly at the time my focus was on money. In January 1992 it was all about to change for me in a massive way. It involved a family and a fire in a small Massachusetts town.

The mom was a third shift nurse, and she went off to work that night and she kissed her kids and husband good night and off she went. Dad was at home with the kids but eventually went to sleep. Little did he realize danger was lurking in the shadows. Apparently, inside the wall there was an electrical fire brewing and the thing about electrical fires is that they require oxygen and so do humans. So, the fire can use all the available oxygen depriving any one in the house of oxygen. With little oxygen sometimes people don't wake up or if they do they are delirious.

This fire was gaining momentum and somebody passing by called the fire department. It was late at night and so by the time the fire department got there they began kicking open doors and windows. The fire department discovered the dad passed out by the door and laid out behind him were his three-year-old and two-year-old children. Remember, mom is a third shift nurse working and little does she realize that her babies and love of her life are in a life-threatening situation. She has no idea what is going on. So, the fire department gets dad onto the sidewalk and begins the revival efforts and they actually revive dad right on the sidewalk.

They are attempting to revive the two children. Imagine that you're the dad and you're on the sidewalk and you come to and you realize what is going on what is your first thought? Where are my kids? As the dad looked off in the distance he noticed the firemen and the paramedics trying to revive his two little babies. Moments later he discovered that his little three-year-old and two-year-old didn't make it.

Can you imagine the devastation that this man was dealing with going through this? Can you imagine the devastation mom experienced when she learned that her two babies passed away in this fire? Friends I can only tell you this, this incident had such a profound impact on me that my alarm sales business now became a crusade, and I was never the same. Later the nephew of these people actually came to work for my company,

so I got the inside track of what took place, and it was just pure devastation. This only further fueled my mission. As a result I developed a ridiculous passion for fire safety and selling Alarm Systems.

I look back on my own story of being faced by my own limitations and overcoming the pain of when Mike asked me to leave the company or take less money. Looking back, I realize the reason I didn't give up that day was because of the impact this story had on me. So, when I took less money after Mike's ultimatum I had the passion and purpose inside of me. I was now on a crusade to never allow this to happen to someone again if I could avoid it.

My own personal closing ratio ascended rapidly to the 70-80% mark on a $3,200 average sale and with a five year monitoring contract for $25 per month. But then I started teaching others how to do what I now knew and how to do it; and then, through the efforts of my sales teams, I went on to sell tens and tens and tens and tens and tens and tens of thousands of Alarm Systems and as a result, made millions and millions and millions and millions of dollars.

Allow me to summarize. There is a purpose to your sales career. It is your job to get clear on this and to allow that to be your NorthStar to keep you focused. In the next chapter I'm going to assist you in rounding out that purpose with what I call a *Healthy View Of Selling*. When you put these two pieces together you have very powerful pillars which will support you in serving your market and generating wealth.

Be mindful of what it is you're selling. Are you expanding in that product or are you contracting? If you are expanding, excellent. If you are contracting, why? Is it because you don't belong selling the product or is there a limitation inside of you that needs to be overcome? In other words, is it a roadblock or a detour? You have to go in to discover these answers and a little coaching from someone who has some wisdom wouldn't hurt you either.

Proverbs 15:22

"Without counsel plans fail, but with many advisors they Succeed"

This explains why looking back on my career I can see where my struggle was when I got in the car sales. I was taking the guidance from my friend Joe and he was making a lot of money. When I got into insurance sales I was coming from fear and I didn't get any guidance and I struggled. Then I got into the Alarm Systems business with the guidance of my mentor Mike and my career went to new heights. Not only did it go to new heights, but I found my purpose, I found my field of favor and my crusade. So it is my wish and prayer that you as a reader would find your field of favor. I am sending that energy to you through these pages that you would get the clarity so that you can build your sales into the masterpiece that I know it is capable of becoming.

Action Step

What is my true purpose? What is it that I think about all of the time? How can I act on this? How can I share this? By when?

CHAPTER 3

Sales Profit Philosophy

"Your Words, Energy and Actions all emanate from your philosophy"
~ Mark Tosoni

Notes & Ideas

CHAPTER 3

Sales Profit Philosophy

Going back to my car sales days we would actually sell rust proofing and paint shield to customers. And I can remember after a customer would leave running around high-fiving people if we sold what we called "The Full Package." At the time, the energy behind this was an energy of doing something to people not for them and although I participated in the sales behavior I never felt good about it. The ability to influence others is a big responsibility bigger than you realize. I could only tell you this, throughout my career I have made many, many millions but I also want you to know I have lost over seven figures in bad investments, bad loans or any other weird ways that you can lose money.

"For whatsoever a man Soweth that shall he also reap" - Galatians 7:7-9

We've all heard the saying *"What goes around comes around"* and *"What you put out comes back".* There are all sorts of sayings in our culture to depict this simple truth. I would ask and invite you to contemplate the responsibility you have as a person of influence. I can promise whatever you put out with bad intention or with an intention of getting over on someone, because perhaps you have a belief that says I don't trust people or people are not safe therefore I'm going to do things to people not for them, this will come back to you and you will not like the consequences.

Here's what I've learned from my experience back in those car sales days and through observations of salespeople for over three decades. I'd like to introduce you to what I call ***The Sales Profit Philosophy***, which essentially is a healthy view of selling. When you learn the sales profit philosophy and you implement this into your business you will become a force to be reckoned with. You will have an advantage over other sales reps who are in house or other businesses that you might be going up against.

The advantage at times seems unfair. As of my writing this book, the sales of my company that I am a partner in are exceeding $60 million a year. My real estate continues to grow and blossom and become more profitable. And of course, the third leg of my stool; Mark, the Speaker, Author and Coach, is also prospering as my books and writings are traveling worldwide and having an impact around the globe. This has been my intention for many, many years to assist sales driven entrepreneurs in accessing their true self and their full potential. The way you access your true self and full potential is to sell from a place of serving and solving people's problems and goodness will come back to you. It will be overflowing. You will not be able to contain it. This is my prayer and my wish for you as my reader so long as you agree with that.

So, let me explain what a healthy view with selling is. It is a great privilege and honor to bring you these teachings. This is the foundation of your career from here forward. If you build your foundation on this rock it will stand in a storm. If you build it in sand it will blow away when the winds of change come, so be receptive now. I cordially invite you to accept these teachings into your mind into your body and into your spirit, *Here We Go...*

#1
Discover People's Needs And Wants

I once heard it said,

> *"If you can sell John Smith through John Smith's eyes, you can sell John Smith what John Smith buys."*

It's always amazed me observing other salespeople through the years how few of them have a process to discover people's needs and wants to really understand what their problems are related to your product. So many salespeople have given the business of sales a bad name and a bad reputation because they fail at this simple step to understand what people's needs, desires and problems are related to your solution. You've got two things here:

A. What are their needs or the problem they have. This is the responsibility of you, the salesperson, to discover what their problem is and to solve their problem, to address their pain to make their pain go away.

B. This has to do with what they want, what are they moving towards, what and how would they like to solve what they are moving towards, can you help them solve it, are you clear on how to solve it, etc.

You see this comes down to *Situational Awareness.* It's kind of difficult to put that in a box because all people are different, each presentation is different, but at the same time they are painstakingly similar.

If you do not have a process to discover people's needs and wants, know this, you will by the end of this book and you will learn a step-by-step process for this in an upcoming chapter. In the meantime, I want you to make it your intention to want to know what are your people's needs and wants are?

So many sales people really don't care, they just go into an appointment, a demo, a home or business or a phone call, with the intention that I'm selling today. And I think you have to have that intention, but at the same time it's important that you have a greater intention that says,

> *"I'm here to serve, I'm here to solve, and once I serve and once I solve then I have earned the right to sell."*

The definition of a high-pressure sales person Is this,

> *"I don't know people's needs and wants nor do I care, yet I try to close the sale anyways"*

Remember what you sow is what you will reap; that's exactly what will come back to you. So the intention is to go in to serve, to solve and then to sell and we do this by discovering people's needs and we do this by discovering people's desires.

#2
Fill Their Needs And Wants

So now that you're clear on what your customer desires and what they need, now it is your job through your product or service to fulfill their needs and wants through your offer. So, the question becomes does your product really solve their needs and wants in a spectacular way? Or does your product solve their needs in an average way?

Does your product solve their needs and wants in a spectacular way, but you are only explaining it in an average way? Or do you explain it in a spectacular way, but your product really only solves it in an average way?

The good news is this, if you do not know how to explain your offer in a spectacular way you will learn how through these pages. However, if your product only solves their problems in an average way you or your company should consider retooling your offer so that it solves their problem in spectacular fashion. This will increase your conversions exponentially just by having the intention and desire to fill their needs and wants and then if your offer matches your intention by solving the problem in spectacular fashion you are going to outperform your competition by a long shot. There are mistakes I made in the Alarm Systems business that I have of course corrected in the solar sales and installation company that I own and this is one of them, having a unique offer that truly solves their problem.

A friend of mine is in the scrap metal business; his name is Mike Melio. Some of you might know him because he's a regular speaker on the Tony Robbins seminar circuit. Mike retooled his company which essentially buys companies' scrap metals and then sells them. What he discovered was that often the companies he was soliciting to do business with had people inside the company who were stealing scrap metal from their employer. So Mike came up with a solution and knocked this out of the park.

Number One, he offers each and every one of his customers a camera system that stares at the scrap metal bins; none of his competitors do this.

Number Two, he gives them a special way to weigh the scrap metal so that they know they are not being ripped off by their employees or him; total transparency. The end result? Mike is one of the leading scrap metal companies in the country and he is a mega success. You can view him on YouTube by searching Mike Melio and Tony Robbins you will see him in an interview with Piers Morgan, pretty cool. Mike and I have been friends since 1992.

#3
Do It In A Win-Win Way

There are many well-known sales trainers who, to this day, just don't get the point of a win-win situation; it is not important in their world. Business is an environment to be dominated and that's it. Now, I do not disagree that business is an environment that is competitive and that you should strive to outperform your competition, but should this be done at the expense of the customer or the consumer? Is your product offering ecological? In other words, is it good for the company? Is it good for the environment? Is it good for the economy? Is it good for the customer and, is it good for you? Is it good for everyone involved? Does it produce and generate a win-win for everyone?

The Law Of Life

When I learned this law many years ago my whole career changed. The law of life basically states, "more life." So, if you can really focus on bringing more life into everything you do, you automatically align with the laws of the universe and you begin to expand. If you neglect the laws of the universe or you don't know them due to ignorance you will contract. I'm speaking to you about a serious universal law, the law of life. This will greatly impact your career in unseen ways and will seemingly give you an unfair advantage over anyone else who speaks to your customer.

People will gravitate to you and they will want to do business with you because they will pick up on the energy. The arrogance of some people in business to think they are outsmarting others by using manipulative tactics to outsmart others for their own gain. You might as well just go be a freaking thief or a politician. You think it's not going to come back around to you in some other way? If you don't, you clearly have not figured out the laws of the land that I am presenting you. So, when you present an offer to somebody, do it in a win-win way, make sure everyone is walking away a winner.

There are certain people in my own company that I noticed from time to time trying to slide one past the company. Other people from time to time try to slide one past the customer. At the end of the day you should never try to slide anything past anyone. Everything you ever do comes right back to you; when will you learn? This is for those with ears to hear, open your ears, open your spiritual ears, what you do to others you do to yourself. The truth is, in spirit we are all connected. When you understand this great spiritual truth your career will ascend to levels you may have never even imagined.

#4
Add Tons Of Value

What does it mean to add tons of value? This can be done on many levels. Earlier I talked about how my friend Mike Melio handles that in the scrap metal business, you might want to ask yourself,

> *"What are my intangibles that I could offer to my customer that would get me a lot more business?"*

One of the intangibles that I use in my business to add more value, believe it or not, is all that we've been talking about up until this point. We often say to customers,

> *"Listen, we're all human and we make mistakes, but we care like no other and we will follow through relentlessly till the end until you are a raving fan."*

We don't just say this, we back it up. Currently my company is ranked number one out of the top 100 solar companies in the United States for positive reviews; number one as of this writing. I'm not just saying it, I have to live it. That's one way we add tons of value. Another way to add tons of value is simply by caring about a customer going into the business transaction with the intention to serve using the five components of a healthy view of selling, this in itself adds tons of value.

There are many other areas where you can add value. Speed adds value, bonuses can be added as a value add, free equipment can be a value add, special discounts could be a value and to a customer or some other form of promotion.

Let me give you an example. My realtor, Brian, sold me my North Carolina home and he used to be one of my salesmen. I recruited him in a parking lot of a car dealership when he was in his early 20s. He went on to become a real estate agent and broker and he's really good at it. One of his intangibles that I urged him to do is to write a book about his experiences, which he has yet to do by the way (Brian if you're reading, write that book). It is what I call, "The million-dollar Rolodex."

When I got to Charlotte, I didn't know anybody, and Brian had painters, he had air conditioning people, he had pool people, he had roofers, he had interior designers for anything that I needed, he had a person. I've urged him to write a book called Brian's million-dollar Rolodex because, what a value add that is to somebody moving into a new city. It's intangible knowledge that would become tangible if he turned it into a book. What a great way to help someone else and to differentiate yourself.

Another way to add massive value is by learning the process to discover people's needs and wants so that you more clearly understand what is important to them. If you can clearly understand what they need and want and what the problems are that they are looking to solve, it makes it a lot easier for you to solve that problem, whatever the problem is. You've also got to really listen with the intention to understand what their situation is. When you do, they will absolutely pick up on this and will feel safe with you. They will pick up on your desire to help them and they will intern want to reciprocate and do business with you. This is how it works, it's actually really simple, it's only difficult if you are hyper focused on your own needs or your personal self-interest. You have to find a way to transcend your own needs to be able to take care of the needs of the consumer in front of you, when you do that, it's a new game.

#5
Express Yourself Through A Product You Love

This section of this chapter is sort of self-explanatory, however it is not always obvious. When I got into the Alarm Systems business I loved the fact that I had a mentor who helped me, and then the fire happened that I spoke of earlier. In the story, I told you about how it put me on a mission, on a crusade and then something else happened in 1993.

One day my mentor told me you will be doing the sales training tomorrow. At the time we had 45 salespeople and I did my best to put together my thoughts and ideas. Then our Wednesday sales meeting came around and I was there bright and early and when the time came my mentor called me up in front of the group and I started to share with them what I knew. I suddenly realized in that moment as I captivated 45 adults most of which were older than me at the time that I had a wealth of information to teach and somehow I was good at this. My passion went even deeper. Now I'm in a business with a mentor who I couldn't be happier to learn from, I'm in an industry that I'm on a crusade to save lives and now I get to train and teach people and help them avoid the pitfalls that I went through making their journey a little easier than mine. I was left with only one question; how can it get even better than this?

Although I didn't expect it at the time, it was only a few years later that I started writing books. My first book, ***Sell Like Crazy Without Going Insane***. My second book, ***Fast Strategies for Maximum Influence***. My third book, ***Six-Figure Commission Sales Secrets***. And finally I wrote about everything I knew about the alarm business and how to sell alarms, I wrote the book ***Alarm Sales Mastery***. And now, ***Mark Tosoni's No Close, Close***.

Friends I can only tell you, find a way to express yourself through a product you love even if you have to be the one to create the product. All I know is every time I engage in writing books and coaching somehow my primary business expands and when my primary business expands I have more money to invest in real estate and my residual income continues to grow and expand.

So now after many years my three-legged stool is working synergistically together. My question to you is,

> *"Do you love the product you're selling, are you expressing yourself through a product you love? Or are you in a product just to make money and get by?"*

If you're in a product just to make money and get by, you're shorting yourself, shorting your family, shorting the market and shorting the universe.

I want to share a principal with you, you are paid in direct proportion to the value you add. If you would like to be paid or compensated more you must find ways to add more value, if you do not love your product, you will not be inclined to add more value.

My prayer and my wish for you is that you will be inspired to add value; to solve people's pain and to fix problems in the marketplace of your choosing. The last thing I want to say is make sure the market you're in is hungry. If you are trying to solve problems expressing yourself through a product you love but there's no pain in that market to be solved you will likely go hungry. So, it's massively important to express yourself through a product you love, but it is also important that the market you are dealing with is a starving crowd. *See you in the next chapter.*

Action Step

Write down the *Sales Profit Philosophy* on an index card, place it in your car where you can see it on the way to your appointments!

CHAPTER 4

Rapid Rapport Riches

"Rapport equals trust, plus comfort."

~ Neil Strauss

Notes & Ideas

CHAPTER 4

Rapid Rapport Riches

I'm super excited to get into this topic of building rapport because it truly is the essence of sales. Without it, nothing happens. With it, you quickly and easily become the trusted advisor. I think it was Dr. Stephen Covey that said in his book ***The Seven Habits of Highly Effective People***,

> *"Seek first to understand, then to be understood."*

Wow! Has this been a driving force of my business career! I've not always done a good job at this. More often than not, I've done a poor job, but I always had the correct intention to help people and serve. Someone once said, *"The road to destruction is paved with good intentions."* This might be partially true, however I didn't always have the best skill set when it came to building rapport. Intention will carry you through because people feel your energy. They're wired to know when to protect themselves and when to let their guard down. In this chapter I will give you distinctions to assist you in helping people to let their guard down so they'll at least listen to what you have to say.

In the introduction I talked about missing my first 11 demos in a row and on my 12th demo I made the decision that I was not leaving the house without a sale. What I decided to do was to go in there and get these people to absolutely fall in love with me. I spent two hours just shooting the breeze with these people and we had a good ol' time. You could see their guard was down and at the time I did have the intention to serve and make a difference, but my overarching intention was to make money. Somehow these people sensed the goodness in me and by the end of the demo they said, "Yes," and I sold my first alarm.

The first idea I want to share with you in this chapter is that **The Goal Of Rapport** is to form a connection. The definition of rapport is a close, harmonious relationship in which the people or groups concerned understand each other's feelings or ideas and communicate well. So really focus on the goal of rapport and focus on the definition of rapport and make this your goal to accomplish this in every business interaction you encounter.

What would prevent somebody from having or holding this intention? It's really simple, and we already touched on this. There is a belief that says,

> *"I don't trust people, people are not safe, or people will hurt me."*

If you've not already dealt with these beliefs I would recommend you release and let them go and replace them with more empowering beliefs such as,

> *"People are generally good. People are conspiring to support me and do right by me. People are safe, I love people."*

The invitation is for you to level up your beliefs system around people and you will be more likely to want to connect with them and serve them.

What I'm going to share with you now is a concept that you will never see in the sales game. The reason you don't typically see this in the sales game is because it comes out of therapy. One of the things I do a lot to look to other areas to pull strategy and technique that will be effective in the game of sales. What I'm about to share with you is extremely powerful when you recognize the power and implement it. It will change your life and you will come to love this as a strategy because it will give you an unfair advantage.

Welcome to the Ways Of Being!

There are four primary ways of *Being* that people are in. When you can recognize these ways, you can speak to them and you can suddenly adapt your presentation and your conversation to really speak this person's language. I'm going to give you the overview in the book and I have to say that these ways of being require coaching to really help you master them. Of course, if you ever want to coach with me you can simply go to

(www.tmarktosoni.com/coachwithmark) and sign up for my year-long coaching program. It will change your life and double your sales.

OK, let's get back to the ***Ways Of Being.***

Our First Way Of Being is what we call Knowing.

A knowing person has a few interesting characteristics. Number one, they live for safety. These types of people have a need for certainty, safety, security and all goes better for them when they know ahead of time. They really like control and they like routines. They get great comfort from knowing they literally crave certainty and knowing.

The Second Way Of Being is Spontaneity.

The spontaneous person is the opposite of knowing. These people live for change and aliveness. They need change, variety and spontaneity. They don't like the humdrum; they don't like routine or consistency and most of the time they literally get a positive rush from not knowing.

The Third Way Of Being is Recognition and Acknowledgment.

A recognition and acknowledgment person likes to be significant and likes to feel important. They need to experience themselves as, *"I am important."* They like to experience themselves as powerful, special, unique or as the best in order to feel good. The unique characteristics about a recognition and acknowledgment person is that they put "I" or "me" before "we." This doesn't make them bad; this is just how they do it.

The Fourth Way Of Being is Closeness.

A closeness person is very different from a recognition and acknowledgment person. These people have to allow love and connection to rule their lives. They need to be connected to others and need to experience closeness. They need to have a loving connection in order to feel like life is working for them. Without love and connection, they're not going to function very well. These people put the "we" before the "I" and they're big socializers and love affection.

I'm going to give you an Action Step here because it's as far as we can go in a book on this topic. I wanted to introduce you to the ways of being because these have not been talked about before in the world of selling:

I want you to figure out your two top ways of Being and I want you to focus on these for 30 days. I want you to just contemplate daily,

> *"Who am I and what are my top two ways of being?"*

Once you clearly understand how you are and who you are you will be so much better at understanding who others are. It was Aristotle who said,

> *"Knowing yourself is the beginning of all wisdom."*

This is very true. Most sales professionals never take the time to know who they are and therefore they are usually a big pile of unmet needs. When you have unmet needs, you will typically be a taker versus when you know who you are, and your needs are met you will become a giver. You will become a person who can serve. So, this awareness in this teaching of ways of being is one of the most powerful things you can do to elevate your sales career.

I can tell you that since I've had this distinction, my income has increased radically because I am able to connect to and influence people at a much deeper level which produces profound increases in results. Here's a shameless plug.

> Coach with me and you will learn all about the ***Ways Of Being,*** and beyond, which will translate into massive increases in your performance.

I'll now share a story with you to bring this chapter home, entitled *"John, the Mechanic."* So, there was this guy who has an old 57' Chevy and it was running like garbage so he brought it down the street to a garage and asked the owner if he could take a look at it. The owner took a look at it and told him he won't be able to fix it because he doesn't know a thing about fixing old cars. So, he brought the car down the road to another mechanic only to be told the same thing. Frustrated, he called a friend and this friend recommended that he visit John, a very good mechanic on the other side of town.

So off he went and met John. John went under the hood for a few minutes and then asked the guy to run it around the block and tell him how it's running. He did and when he came back, told John,

"I don't know what you did but this thing is running amazing!"

John called him to the counter and gave him the bill. The bill was $500 which surprised the Chevy owner. He muttered, *"Wow John, that's a lot of money! I mean you were under the hood for only a couple of minutes!"* To this John replied, *"Correct, I was under the hood for only a couple of minutes, but it took me 30 years to figure out which screws to turn."*

My friends, do not underestimate the *Power Of This Teaching*. It took me 30 years to learn how to earn a deep level of trust and rapport with people. You can shorten that learning curve exponentially and that is the benefit of reading books and coaching with experts - we shave your learning curve so that you can impact a whole lot more people in way less time and generate way more revenue in a shorter amount of time.

The next idea is called ***Matching and Mirroring***. This also comes from therapy and is much more popular. This has been around for a long time and was derived from the late great therapist's work, Milton Erickson, a master in rapport building. He would use his rapport building skills to break people free from phobias and psychological issues that no one else could in record time. Two men by the name of Richard Bandler and John Grinder we're fascinated with the work of Erickson and decided to study him and copy his best practices. Their work became known as NLP or Neuro-linguistic programming and is said to be the fastest and best technology in the personal development world. I have studied NLP extensively and I have used it throughout my sales career. I have found that when it is paired with positive intent and a healthy view of selling, it will have tremendous results. I have also discovered that if it is used to manipulate it's better to not use it at all. That is my warning to you.

Here's how it works; just look at the words, *Match and Mirror or, Reflect.* It's a very interesting phenomenon because when you match and mirror or reflect people on three primary levels (physiology, tonality, rate of speech), you step into the customers' experience and you begin to see the world through their eyes more so than if you were to not use matching and mirroring.

Again, suppose you're coming with positive intent and you want to understand what people are experiencing. In that case, you can get very good at this. I've noticed the people who get very good at this do so because they have a strong desire to serve and to assist other people. I've also noticed that people who try to use it to manipulate are put off and shut down, so proceed with caution.

Matching And Mirroring Physiology

Back in my car sales days, one of the early lessons I learned was to take my hand during a handshake and turn it on top of the person's hand that I was shaking and squeeze hard. I never quite understood this, but I was told this was used to obtain control. Even from the earliest days, I began studying NLP and it taught something very contrary, that is, to copy people's physiology.

So, I came up with an idea to apply what I learned that I came to call, *"The Identical Handshake."* I thought to myself if copying people's physiology helped us get rapport why not copy their physiology right from the handshake so that when they shook my hand it would feel the same as their hand. I have absolutely no scientific research about this, I only know that I was very good at getting rapport and I believed that the identical handshake is where it began so you can use that if you wish.

What I aimed to do when I went into a sales appointment was to match and mirror their hand motions, what they did with their hands or arms, how they set the entire angle of their body, so while I was warming up with my conversation with them, I would merely copy their body language. Sometimes I would begin with the husband and I would move to the wife, other times I would move to the wife and go back to the husband. It's a very intuitive process when you're with two people and you are matching and mirroring both of them. I'll show you how you can tell if you already have rapport or not.

If we were sitting at a table and they have their left leg crossed over the right leg, I would just do the same. If their arms are down in their lap, I'll just keep my arms down in my lap as well. I'll pay attention to their subtle body movements and gestures, and I will do my best to merely reflect those gestures and movements little by little. You begin to feel what the customer is feeling depending on how sensitive and intuitive you are. This gives you a great advantage because you understand the customer's state. As soon as you do, your next move is to pull them out of their state and move them into the state you want them to be in.

Next, I would,

Match And Mirror Tonality

Right from the greeting when I did the identical handshake, I would say, *"Hi, my name is Mark."* I do this in a very positive way just over the neutral line, trying to listen to their tone. If I were with a senior citizen, I might lower my voice and if I were with someone louder, I would raise it. You quickly read their tone and when they say something back then you just copy that as well. So now you are copying the handshake, you are copying their physiology when you're sitting and talking with them and now you are copying their tonality so what ends up happening here on an unconscious level is their mind says, *"Oh, this person is like me!"*

People tend to trust people they find similarities with so they are more receptive to you. This will work powerfully if you practice it and master it. The irony of it is that I've never had anyone look at me and say, *"Hey Mark, are you Matching And Mirroring me?"* Of course, if they did, I would say,

> *"Absolutely, it's very important that we get rapport so that I can get you the results you're really looking for and so yes, I use matching and mirroring as a strategy to get there."*

There would be no sense in denying it when I intend to be there to help them.

Lastly, we will,

Mirror Speech Rate

And I don't mean their tonality in volume but rather, how fast they speak. If you are in the South, you might notice that people speak a little slower. If you are in the North, you might notice they speak a little faster. This has zero connection with intelligence. This has everything to do with the culture they were raised around. It's also important to know and to notice that certain people just naturally speak faster. If the person is more visually oriented, they tend to see things in their mind very quickly so there is a tendency to speak faster. This is one way you'll know you're with a visual person. If the person is predominantly auditory, they speak at a mid-range - not too fast, not too slow. And if the person is kinesthetic, one of the ways you'll know is they tend to speak very slowly because they're processing things in their body.

As sales professionals, it's important for us to start to tune into the subtleties with our prospects so they can more easily become customers. Once you have a rapport, even if it's on an unconscious level for the customer, they will begin to like you, and won't know why. They will feel like you are very similar to them, which causes them to feel safe which drops their guard and unconsciously translates to, *"I'm giving you permission to be my trusted advisor instead of Google,"* which is exactly what you want to happen. That said, most of this chapter could be researched on your own except for the ways of being (you won't find those anywhere because that's part of my secret stash). The matching and the mirroring can be found on YouTube, and of course, if you want to master these strategies, join me and coach with me in my one-year program and you will gain mastery over all these and way more.

Action Step

Where could you begin to match and mirror in your demo? By when will you?

CHAPTER 5

The Power of Invisible Influence

"Never underestimate the influence you have on others."

~ Laurie Buchanan

Notes & Ideas

CHAPTER 5

The Power of Invisible Influence

It was 1993, and I'm in the house of what looked like the man from the Gorton's fisherman commercial; an old yankee. I'm in a small Connecticut town, and I presented to my prospect and his wife the numbers, and his reaction was, *"I haven't made a one-day decision ever in the 72 years of my life."* They liked me, liked the company, liked the product, and felt like they needed it to a degree, but they were stalling to close the deal. So, what do you do?

As a sales pro, we should make a judgment call in every appointment. Is this right for the customers, and can they afford this? Of course, this could be tricky because buyers will do things to defend themselves financially. I've often spoken of a *"Prearranged Game Plan"* - sometimes, you would think buyers go to buyers' schools to figure out how to say no to offers, LOL. So, in this particular case, I decided that the light was green, and so when the light is green, my motto is, *"Go Sell."*

I am a believer that we must earn the right to sell. I do not care for assumptive selling nor assumptions. That said, what I do like is to get all the necessary chips off the table, so all that's left is the final offer and the close. So, what are those chips to take off the table?

Number One - Do I have a relationship with the customer? A connection? Do I genuinely want to help them, and are they genuinely receptive to the help I can give?

Number Two - Do they need my solution, and does it solve a significant problem?

Number Three - Do they want to solve that problem? Do they have the financial resources to make it happen? If the answer to those questions is all YES, the light is green, then *GO. Go For It,* close the deal, put it together, and make it happen.

Provided the light is green, I'd like to offer some tools to assist you on your path. Side note (which, by the way, takes place through your whole demo), you have to use judgment when you are demonstrating a product or service to someone. If it's not right for them for some reason, you must walk away, just the same when if it is right for them, you should get it done.

The first tool we're going to talk about is what we call the *"Pre-Frame."* This is one of my favorite tools when I write, speak, and sell. Pre-framing essentially is setting the stage for what is to come. Another way to say this is by telling them what you want them to think. Here are a few examples of pre-framing:

> *"In a moment, I'm going to show you my product or service, and if you're like most people, you're going to love it. Most people love it so much that they do cartwheels, so be careful. I don't want you to hurt your back, LOL."*

Another example of pre-framing is something like this:

> *"In a moment, I'm going to talk to you about why so many people go ahead with my product or service and what they all report to me is an overwhelming sense of safety once they go ahead and say Yes."*

Now, in those two pre-frame examples, some other things are going on, which I will point out to you in a few moments but just remember that pre-framing is essentially telling people what you want them to think, telling them in advance what to think. They will merely follow along, and you will gain tremendous confidence in the process. Let me give you one more example:

> *"In a moment, I'm going to show you how this product or service closes that gap, and you're going to be amazed because it works every time because we haven't had a single failure yet."*

You see, you're setting up the frame for what will happen. This is extremely powerful in the game of influence, but this alone is not enough and is merely part of the process.

Next, I want to talk about *Reframing*. Reframing is learning to be great at rebuttals. It's challenging to be in the sales game if you do not know how to do rebuttals. Your job is to move people in a certain direction regarding the way they're thinking about what it is you're offering. If you don't move them in that direction, it's going to result in a no-sale, so you have to learn how to reframe situations. I'll give you a few examples:

It could happen during the prospecting phase or at the beginning of the appointment. Back in the day, when I was running my alarm business, I would go to the appointment, and suddenly my prospect would say,

> *"I thought about the appointment, and I'm no longer interested."*

So, I would reply to their disinterest by saying,

> *"No issue if you're not interested, we understand, and we wouldn't want you to do anything against your will. That being said, can I ask you a question? If you knew for sure that the time you spent with me today might make a difference and save a life down the road, would it have at least been worth listening to?"*

Can you see the reframe in the question? Someone else might say they can't afford it. Again, you must determine whether your customer has the financial resources to be able to invest in your solution to solve their problems. If somebody were to reply,

"I can't afford it," a reframe would be something like this:

> *"Mr. Customer, I understand that this might burden you financially. I've got great news for you, if that's the case I won't even let you go ahead with it. That said, consider this: If you don't do it and the problem continues to escalate and worsen, what would the cost of damage be? I think it's fair to say that the damage would be much larger than to go ahead and make the investment now to solve the problem, Yes?"*

Do you see we are merely reframing here? Now again, these could be used early on as rebuttals and even during the demonstration. Learning how to reframe situations is a *Master Skill.*

Let me give you another example: When the customer says, *"I don't need it,"* you can say,

> *"I understand Mr. Customer, and if you're not comfortable and don't feel that you need it, I've got great news for you. I won't even let you go ahead with it. That said, ask yourself this question: If you wait until the time*

comes that you really need it, what are the consequences that you are likely to face? Doesn't it make sense to take the opportunity now and be prepared should a major problem arise?"

Embedded Commands are one of my favorite things to do in the world. Here is my warning about this tactic - only use embedded commands if you have adopted a healthy view of selling. If not, do not use this. The usage of embedded commands is a very powerful tactic. An embedded command is sort of like a pre-frame built into a sentence so that the conscious mind does not hear it.

If you are a sharp person and you go back and look at my pre- framing and reframing examples, you will notice the embedded commands built into the sentences. This is exactly what will happen to you as you become a practitioner - you just need to believe in it, and you will discover how powerful it is and how it seems like you're not even selling because people just want to buy from you.

So, here we go. My favorite embedded command of all time is this,

"Go ahead with it." Using that in a sentence, we will arrive at something like this,

"In the event, you've decided to go ahead with it, you will experience the following advantages" or "One of the reasons, so many of my customers go ahead with it is because..."

Another one of my favorites when I was still running my alarm business goes like this,

"Even in the unlikely event you choose not to go ahead with it, I'd like to leave you with some information of value."

Now, notice the last sentence. The conscious mind is hearing me say, *"It's OK if you don't go ahead with it,"* but the unconscious mind is hearing, *"Go ahead with it."* This is a key distinction about embedded commands; you are no longer speaking to the gatekeeper, the conscious mind. You are speaking to the unconscious mind which can only say *YES*!

I started to learn hypnotic selling through Dr. Donald Moine. He was an early pioneer in utilizing Neuro-linguistic programming in the field of sales training and, when I was very young, in the game and struggling, I happened to read a book of his entitled Unlimited Selling Power. This book did not just increase the living daylights out of my closing ratio, it changed my life forever!

Combining a healthy view of showing positive intention and rapport building with subliminal or hypnotic selling is the mixed martial arts of the influence and persuasion game and I have never discovered anything more powerful. I am only giving you the basics in this book, otherwise, it's going to be a 500-page book, and nobody will buy it. If you want to learn more and go deeper into these distinctions, go ahead and coach with me, LOL.

Seriously, get in touch with me, you will love the results that you will see in your life!

Another favorite embedded command of mine is, *"Say Yes!"* In fact, for those of you who don't know this, I am a partner in a solar sales and installation company, and one of the very first things I did when we began our adventure was to write a book titled ***Say Yes to Solar***. This is a very common language in my company. My people are taught these tactics and strategies and processes along with ways of being positive intent and rapport building - this is my secret sauce friends, and I'm sharing it all with you here.

Here are a few examples.

> *"Mr. and Mrs. Customer, in the event you say Yes you are going to experience the savings from month one."*

Let me give you another one.

> *"One of the reasons, Mr. Customer, that so many of my customers say Yes is because we haven't had a single failure yet and it works every time."*

You can even combine this, and this where it kind of gets fun. I'll give you an example.

> *"The reasons so many of our customers say Yes and go ahead with it is because..."*

Or, it could go something like this,

> *"Mr. and Mrs. Smith, in the event you absolutely love the solution, and you say Yes and go ahead with it here's what you will notice."*

And then, of course, you can even intensify this in better commands by saying,

> *"Go ahead with this today," or "Say Yes and go ahead with this today."*

See, the idea here is to place the commands inside the sentences and the usage of repetition is subtle. I'd like to give you one more, *"Trust me."*

You must know by now that your customers don't trust you initially. What better way to get them to trust you than to build an incredible rapport with them, show them that you have a positive intention, and then embed commands into sentences that tell them what you want them to do? So this would sound like,

> *"One of the reasons so many of my customers trust me is because I have performed so well for them,"*

Or,

> *"One of the reasons you should trust me is because we have a proven track record and we're currently ranked number one in positive reviews in the United States of America."*

Provided that was true and of course, that is true with my solar company that's why I use that as an example. There's many more and there's no limit to how you can use them as they can be used in rebuttals. You'll notice that I do use them in my reframing, rebuttals, and handling objections and concerns.

Another one of my favorite invisible hypnotic patterns is the future. Sometimes referred to as ***Future Pacing*** or ***Posthypnotic Suggestion***, this is an extremely powerful tool that I have used for years. I've used it primarily to take them into the future so they will know what to expect. One example is this,

> *"One thing you'll know for sure in the event you say yes and go ahead is that your problem will be solved permanently."*

Or this,

> *"One thing you'll know for sure if you say Yes and go ahead with me is you will experience the benefits for many years to come."*

Or another,

> *"If you decide to say Yes and go ahead you will notice after some time that you no longer have this concern."*

In these examples, you are telling them outright what could happen in the future if they say *Yes* to you.

One of my favorite ways to use this is in what we call the *"Button Up."* This is where you test and validate the strength of the sale. So, in the button up we would say something like this,

> *"You might notice that after I leave, you will have a few questions or concerns. All this means is that you are getting ready to save money, so just jot down your concerns, and here's my phone number. Make sure you call me."*

So here in this one, I'm telling them in advance that should they have concerns, they can immediately call me. I have been teaching this for many years, and I would take total amateurs with no sales experience whatsoever and have them up and running and selling lots and lots of products in as little as a week. Often times, I won't even tell them what was under the hood of the car - it's just part of the sales scripting process. I have a saying that an organized demo is first, a science, and then it becomes an art. I am a big believer in an organized demonstration, strategically utilizing words and phrases to persuade and influence prospects as long as it's all with positive intent and incredible rapport.

Action Step

Write a Pre-Frame. Write a Reframe. Write an Embedded Command. Write a Post Hypnotic Suggestion.

CHAPTER 6

Telling Is Not Selling

"We live in an age of distrust, lead people with powerful questions. Allow them to draw their own conclusions."

~ Mark Tosoni

Notes & Ideas

CHAPTER 6

Telling Is Not Selling

In early 1992, after watching my mentor sell 25 Alarm Systems in a row, he handed me the demo book and said *"Get To It"*. I did the demo, and I was as mechanical as I could be, and we missed the sale. I missed all the key components in the demo, and when we finally got back into the car, he told me, *"If you ever do something like that again, I will kill you."* Back then I just thought that the demonstration was some mechanical thing that you did. I was so focused on the mechanics that I forgot all about the philosophy of selling and where my focus should be directed.

Every sales presentation should have a salesperson that understands how to recognize people's needs and wants. The entire sale is built on understanding how to solve a problem and what the customer's desires are. For people to miss this important key concept in creating a sale is a very wrong move.

Over the years, I realized how important this was and in 1995, after I sold my alarm company for pennies on the dollar - the one I was telling you that we sabotaged, the market shifted and we started to give away Alarm Systems for free just to sign up monitoring agreements. So, what I did at the time was I began to work on creating a fast demo. The reason for this was because the system was free. In the past, we would spend two hours doing a demonstration so what I wanted to do was condense the demo. This way we could get to the table with the price quicker and I actually succeeded at this improved demo and this worked well.

One of the processes that I created during this time was what I call ***"The Hot Button Process"*** built with some serious influence and persuasion tactics. I have also discovered that you could apply this to whatever it is you're selling. The interesting thing about the process is it is universal so it could easily be applied to any product or service and so let me share this with you now.

CURRENT UPDATE: I've applied this process to my own solar company, and we are crushing it! The reps continually report how much they like it and how it gives them confidence and the customer clarity, resulting in more sales.

The Hot Button Process

Ask the Question. Had we not offered this special promotion? This free demonstration and this no-cost estimate? What would've been your main motive, to go ahead and purchase would've been due to A, B, C, or D. In other words, if you did it, why would you do it?

So, I want to break down the question for you and then I want to use this question in the context of an alarm system as a case study so you can apply it to your business. First, let me break down the process.

Step One

Had we not offered. What this is doing is just merely setting up the question, then you insert whatever it is you're offering, what would've been your main motive. This elicits the hot button by asking this question. This way, it asks them, *"What is your main motive to go ahead and purchase?"* whatever it is you're selling. Notice in the question is an embedded command, *"Go ahead and purchase."* Then you move into, *"Would it have been due to A, B, C, or D?"* In other words, if you did it, why would you do it?

Now I'm going to give you the actual question, which I used in my alarm business for the hot button process for many, many years, which yielded great success. I've done training with ADT, the nation's largest security company and its dealer program. I teach the same question and it works like magic every single time. That's how powerful this is.

Hot Button Question

> *"Had we not offered our special promotion, what would've been your main motive to go ahead and purchase security today? Would it have been due to due to burglary, robbery, fire, medical emergencies, remote view cameras, or automatic door locks. In other words, if you did it, why would you do it?*

I want you to spend time understanding the question because this is a part of your process after you've warmed up and built a rapport with your customer but before the actual demo. Please allow me to show you how to handle it when the customer answers the question. So, in the question,

> *"Had we not offered our special promotion, what would've been your main motive to go ahead and purchase security today? This can be due to burglary, robbery, fire, medical emergencies, remote view cameras, or automatic door locks. In other words, if you did it, why would you do it?*

Customer response:

"Well, burglary and robbery."

Step Two

Ask, *"Why are these things so important to you?*

Customer response:

"My husband is a traveling salesman and I'm concerned while I'm home at night and when I'm here during the day with the kids."

Then Probe deeper.

"Fantastic! And do you have any other concerns?"

Customer response:

"Well I really would like a camera at the front door, so I don't have to go to the front door. If the doorbell rings, I can just look at my cell phone and see who's there."

Response: *"Okay, great!"*

Step Three

Mirror it back with the ultimate pre-frame and say this,

"So here's what I'm going to create for you. I'm going to design a system that takes into account your concern when your husband is traveling and not at home and, I'm also going to build this system in such a way that during the day when you're here with the kids never again will you have to even remotely worry. Not only that I'm going to propose our Super-

duper Special Door Cams. This way, in the event you choose to go ahead with this, you will feel incredibly safe, and you are going to love it!

So I ask you to look at that last sentence in Step Four because I'm mirroring back to her everything she told me, and then when I'm done with that, I give her the power by putting the *Guard Down* phrase *"In the event,"* then I go on to use an *Embedded Command* choose to go ahead with it" along with a *Preframe, "You are going to love it!"*

I told you this was mixed martial arts, punchs in bunches, not to mention kicks, ground game, taekwondo, etc. It is very powerful, and it's only four simple steps and can be adapted to any other offer. I'm going to pretend here that you sell life insurance and I'm going to show you how I would adopt this in the life insurance business. Here we go!

Life Insurance Adaptation of the Hot Button Process

Step One

"Had we not been out here to discuss your life insurance needs what would've been your main motive to go ahead with life insurance, would it have been due to financial reasons, tax advantages, or a forced savings plan? In other words, if you did it, why did you?"

Customer response:

"Frankly, I'm primarily concerned if something were to abruptly happen to my husband, I would want to know that the kids and I have enough money to get by, especially while we were in a time of grieving."

Step Two

Ask:

> *"And why is something abruptly happening to your husband so important to you?"*

Customer response:

> *"Well, he is getting older and having a few health challenges. We don't have a lot of money saved, we don't have any insurance, and I don't even know how much money I could make if I got a job."*

Then Probe deeper

Response:

> *"Fantastic, is there anything else?"*

Customer response:

> *"I sort of like the idea of a forced savings plan, that sounds sort of interesting, we've not been very good at saving money so I'd like to learn more about that."*

Step Three

Mirror it back with the ultimate pre-frame

Response:

> *"So, here's what I'm going to design for you. I'm going to design a program that, in the event of your husband's untimely death it would leave you*

with enough money so that you and the kids would be all set financially during your time of grieving and beyond.

Not only that, but I will also make sure the program has a forced savings component to it so you can still make use of it regardless of whether your husband lives or dies. Of course, we hope he lives. You will be saving lots of money this way. In the event you choose to say yes and go ahead with this, you will be protected financially and become bulletproof. Wait until you see it; you're going to love it!"

Again, here I just mirror back exactly what she said to me in my own words. I then informed her that I will design a program, especially for her mirroring back, exactly what was important to her. Then I will use an embedded command and then leave her off with the pre-frame. Then I'm off to my next step in the demo.

So, you see that this ***Hot Button Process*** can be applied to many other products. If you are selling windows,

"Had we not been here doing this window demonstration, what would've been your main motive to go ahead and purchase windows? Would it have been due to your yearning to beautify your home, energy efficiency, ease-of-use, ease of cleaning? In other words, if you decided to go ahead with the windows, why did you?"

If you are selling roofs,

"Had we not been here doing this free roof estimate, what would've been your main motive to put a new roof on this house? Would it have been due to age, leaks, yearning to beautify the home? In other words, if you did choose to go ahead with a new roof, why did you?"

Again, these principles can easily be applied to any product or service that you're selling. You've just got to work and learn the four steps and apply them to your business.

Action Step

Take this three-step template and fill it out so that somewhere before your demo and after your warm-up, you can start asking the hot button questions.

Hot Button Template Step One

Ask the Hot Button Questions...

Had we not (fill in the blank; ______________ met you at the show, set the appointment, knocked on your door, etc.),

What would have been your main motive to go ahead with? (your offer, pest control, life insurance, solar, etc.)

Would it have been due to _________________, _________________, or _______________. In other words if you did it, why would you do it?

Step Two

Listen Mindfully And Probe Deeper.

Why is ______________ (whatever they answered) so important to you?

Customer Examples; Pest Control Example:

Customer: *"When those ants get in my house I crawl in my skin".* Rep Replies: "I hear you. Is there anything else?" Customer; "*Well now that you mention it, roaches also make me crawl in my skin".* Rep Reply; "Understood, is there anything else?" Customer; *"Just knowing while me and the kids are sleeping no critters will get on us".* Rep Replies; "Excellent!"

Step Three

Mirror It Back In Their Language

Rep Replies;

"In a moment I am going to design a pest control solution for you, and here is what you will know for sure... ants getting into your home will no longer be possible, roaches are gone forever, yet most important while you sleep never again will you or the kids need to think about critters and crawl in your skin. They will be gone forever. Wait until you see my solution, you are going to love it. In fact you will now be dancing in your skin, versus crawling in your skin. GOOD or GREAT?

CHAPTER 7

Billion Dollar Strategy of Influence

"Other people's opinions sell better than you, the salesperson"

~ Mark Tosoni

Notes & Ideas

CHAPTER 7

Billion Dollar Strategy of Influence

Wow! I'm excited to bring you to this chapter and I can't imagine how much money and leverage I lost by going years and years without this strategy. You may have heard me talk about it throughout these pages that I look to other industries for strategies and techniques, and then I cross them over into direct sales and commission sales. If you're a speaker, author, coach, service provider, or internet marketer, I'm sure you could learn a thing or two about the way we do things when we're selling in a home. I certainly learned a thing or two from you all.

Two of the things I like and appreciate that online marketers do well is the use of the billion-dollar strategy. I like the way that a lot of online and service providers slide the price in an organized manner when they are about to go for **The Close,** that also pertains to people who sell from the platform.

There are other things I like about these folks, but these two stand out the most.

So, I'm bringing to you things that I know will immediately help you grow your business. The reason why I know that this will be a big help to you is that I use this in my business, and, it works.

I'm constantly looking for small hinges to swing big doors. The billion-dollar strategy is the most underutilized strategy that I've discovered in all kinds of sales, so I'm very excited to share this with you. But before I do, I would like to share a baby version of this billion-dollar strategy and then I'll go to the bigger one.

As you know, I write books and one of the things you'll notice in my books are the testimonials. A written testimonial is not a bad strategy, even if it is very underutilized. At a minimum, I'm recommending that you create a written testimonial strategy to increase your sales.

For example,

> *"Check out what Mrs. Smith had to say about us. She's a great lady and sharp as a tack."*

But at the end of the day, she decided to say, *Yes*, and go ahead with us. And look at what she had to say as to why and then read the testimonial. This is a great way to add an embedded command while telling a bit of a story to set up the testimonial. Another example,

> *"Check out what Mary Jones had to say about us and why she chose to say, 'Yes and go ahead' with us. She had a serious problem with her bike, and we were able to solve it for her rapidly. Look what she has to say about it and why she decided to choose us."*

Here you see the ***Embedded Commands,*** *"Say Yes"* and *"Go ahead with us"* and *"Choose us."* I can tell you that when you start to add things like this to your arsenal, your conversions are going to go up!

There are more ways where you can use these throughout your demo - you can use two or three more and you could save a big one for the close. I might add, female testimonials typically outperform male testimonials so make sure you are using lots of the female ones. If you have someone whom you did business with who is an influencer either locally or with some celebrity status obviously that speaks for itself, you might want to include him or her to your testimonial list.

Why do I call this the billion-dollar strategy? Because the billion-dollar strategy comes out of the infomercial business. They have been doing this for years and earned billions of dollars in sales with this strategy by invoking the assistance of ordinary people usually accompanied by a single celebrity. It is proven and indisputable. I tell you, it will work in any industry; anywhere, anytime. *That's how powerful it is!*

Okay, now let's get down to the ***Billion-Dollar Strategy***.

"Before and after video testimonial."

Incredibly underutilized, most of your competitors are doing nothing with this and the reason for that is because it takes a little bit of time to capture this. However, if you're the type of person who likes to spend time working on your business, this would be a massive investment. I utilize it heavily in my business. And frankly, I wish all my people would use them even more because they are that powerful. And of course, the video testimonial is even more powerful than the written testimonial. Before I finish this, I will show you a way to use video testimonials that puts a single video testimonial on steroids.

Before I go down that road, let's dive into the **Billion-Dollar Strategy.** Again, females are more credible and believable. That doesn't mean you won't use males, it just means that females do better. The idea here is to elicit the way your customers feel about you and your company. Now that you have solved the customers problem, it only needs to be a minute long. They don't need to be drawn out. It can be done on a cell phone. You can simply stand next to them after you request permission, tell them to speak from the heart and guide them. Here's what to say.

> *"Look into the camera and tell my prospects how you feel about doing business with me and my company."*

It's a script.

> *"Mr. Customer, can you look into the camera and tell my prospects how you feel about doing business with me? Please speak from the heart and tell them what it was like before we met and what it's like now."*

You're merely standing next to them allowing them to speak into your camera. The more rapport you have, the more they love you, and the better your video testimonials will be.

That's a very simple script and I can tell you, the more you elicit that feeling from the customer, the more powerful the testimonial is. It might even help if you over-deliver and they cry. If you can capture moments like this, then these testimonials will be very powerful.

THE TESTIMONIAL REEL

Once you have a series of these testimonials, you can put it together to create what they call a **"Testimonial Reel."** This is a very simple job for an experienced video editor. You could probably have one made for $100 - $200 and this thing would make you so much money, it's ridiculous. What it does is it takes the highlights from your video testimonials and breaks them into little six to eight second clips and then puts those clips together and adds music to bring a feel to it. It's sort of like machine-gunning video testimonials so one keeps coming after another.

For example,

Mr. and Mrs. Smith, you catch them right when they're saying,

"I love you so much."

Then you get Mr. and Mrs. Jones saying,

"We saved so much money! We are so grateful to this company!"

Then you get the next customer,

"I shopped six different companies and these guys were the real deal."

Then the next one is saying,

"I checked online, and the reviews are incredible!"

Somewhere in the demo, you can play the reel. It can be done at the beginning of the presentation to frame things and where it's going. It can also be used at the very end while you're starting to price things up. My recommendation would be to use a few video testimonials in the beginning.

Perhaps, a few video testimonials that will validate some key points about your product like it actually does save your money or it actually does protect you in some way or the service was actually tested and it worked somewhere in the middle of the demo. You could use the testimonials as validation and towards the end. Almost no one does this, and if this is joined with a healthy view of selling it will do the selling for you. Now you know why the subheading of this book says ***The Ultimate Sell Without Selling Formula.***

I'm big into leverage and I want you to get as much as you possibly can.

I can tell you in my career that I've done quite well and most people you talk to will tell you they've done quite well. What most of them won't tell you is where and when they did bad. I can tell you, I lost tons and tons of leverage without using this strategy. Sometimes, I hate to even think about it. That's the bad news. The good news is I'm using it like crazy today in my business and it's paying back fantastic dividends.

Side Note: I also use this for recruiting. Some people struggle in the area of recruiting. If that's you or your company, think about how you could use testimonials to assist you in recruiting, not only customer testimonials but employee testimonials. You can view one of my sites to see what my employee testimonials look like and some customer testimonials at: www.door2doorsolar.com

Again, I'm always looking for that edge, that small hinge, that little bit of leverage. At the end of the day, I believe when you shoot and strive for these edges, it's the difference that makes the difference. I may have mentioned briefly my high school hockey story. As a hockey player, I guess you know how important edges are, and if you're running out on the ice with those skates, you are not going to play a good game. Your skates need to be sharpened regularly so they dig into the ice and you get traction. Many of us are losing traction in our careers. Make a decision not to lose traction. If you do, you will be happy, but you must do the work.

POSITIVE REVIEW STRATEGY

One little thing I'd like to add to this chapter is the idea of a positive review strategy. Do you or your company have a positive review strategy? If the answer to this is no, I would invite you to spend some time working on your business and coming up with a plan so that you can build positive reviews. I can't tell you everything I do here in the book because it is proprietary.

However, I will tip you off to the one thing I do that has seriously helped us to become number one in positive reviews out of the top 100 solar sales and installation companies; we hired somebody specifically to do just this. Now if you're a salesperson, you might need to do this for yourself or you could potentially influence your company to do this. And of course, there are numerous services out there that can assist you with this.

Another key point I want to make about positive reviews is this,

"What is your intention? What is the intention of your company?"

If it is not an obsession with customer service, making people happy and following through, I can tell you right now, your sales jobs are going to be more difficult than it needs to be. I'm not telling you to quit your company, but I can tell you this, you better lean on them if they don't have this right. Everyone who searches online today talks to you on the phone and searches you. You're searching for other people. This is just where the business has gone so be certain that you are more than interested in taking care of people and building a great reputation for yourself.

From my perspective, it must be an obsession. This is where we're at with our company. It's a lot of work but it's paying off big because I know that when a customer searches us, they're going to find Ten to One good over bad. It's okay if you have a few complaints. The question is, what did you do about them?

This is the reason why I like the Better Business Bureau because it shows the complaint and whether or not your company was able to resolve it. If you do resolve it, people will know that your company cares. You can get past that, but this is how people purchase today so the invitation is for you to build yourself up into a soldier that cannot be beaten on the battlefield.

Action Step

Can you commit to this? When will you have your *Billion Dollar Strategy* done?

CHAPTER 8

The Dynamic Demo

"People buy on emotion and justify their purchases logically"
~ Unknown

Notes & Ideas

CHAPTER 8

The Dynamic Demo

Sometimes, it takes years of doing the same thing over and over again to notice the small hinges. This chapter is going to be filled with six small hinges that can take your game to the next level. These were all discovered through one of two ways, (**1**) by being in house selling or (**2**) helping others who were in house selling to be better at it. It's all field-tested and results approved. You will notice distinctions here you may not have noticed before so take notice. What you're about to learn will forever change your sales career. You are going to demo at 10 levels up from where you are currently positioned.

The interesting thing about this book and about a lot of the books that I write is that you can take from them single strategies and implement them into your game, sort of like a smorgasbord. It's the same here with this chapter. These small hinges can be used or added in any order you'd like anywhere in your demo that you see fit because these are timeless strategies of influence. Remember the *"John, The Mechanic"* story? Well, here we go. Let me show you which screws to turn.

Solve Their Problem!

First and foremost, when you're demoing a product or service, whether tangible or intangible, be mindful that you are now showing them how to solve their problem through the product. So if you didn't clarify earlier what their needs and desires were through the Hot Button Process, and other strategic questions, your product is only generically solving problems, not specifically. So distinction #1 is to solve their problems specifically and hold the intention to discover and solve their problems specifically in regards to your product or service offering.

I Am Here with This Customer to Solve Their Problems First and Foremost!

So what does this look like? Well, go back to the hot buttons; think about what was important to your customer. Let's say, for example, it's new windows for the home. The customer has now revealed that leaky, drafty windows, and energy loss are their big concerns. When you do your demo, it's the time to solve that concern through the features and benefits of your product specifically to the way they described it.

The second big distinction is to have your feature set laid out ready for demonstration. If you have something visual and tangible, that's even better.

FEATURE SET TEMPLATE

The offer:

NO MORE BUGS ULTIMATE PEST CONTROL

Safe And Non Toxic

Perimeter System

100% Bug Free Guarantee

Proven Trap And Destroy Technology

Trained And Certified Technicians

Over 10,000 Bug Free Customer

Fill in your features (explain benefits and feeling using voice inflection and physiology)

Feature #1

Feature #2

Feature #3

Feature #4

Let's say one of your features is the *"Super Duper Window Frame with Advanced Sealing Technology"* in the installation. *(Yes, I'm making this up)*

Window Feature - Super Duper Window Frame With Advanced Sealing Technology.

> *"Mr. and Mrs. Customer, this window is a super-duper window frame with advanced sealing technology. This is what it does, it eliminates drafty windows making your home more comfortable, which saves you money on electricity (benefit), leaving you feeling good about your home and even better, in the event you say Yes to these new windows."*

So, the pattern goes like this: **Feature, Benefit, Feelings (FBF)**. Speak in benefits and feelings.

Through the years, I've watched salespeople with a very serious sales virus which I've come to call *"featuritis."* This sales virus is fatal to a full pocket. But there is a remedy, and it is to learn how to speak in benefits and feelings. Ultimately, people buy benefits and feelings or they purchase results for pain elimination. What benefits and feelings does your product create? What results does your product generate?

Action Step

Create a feature set template for YOUR product/service.

Stack The Benefits

When describing your product, it's important to learn to become a wordsmith, but words are not the most powerful form of influence. Some studies say that words only influence people at around 7%, voice inflection is at 38% while physiology is greatly responsible for like 55%.

Have you ever watched stand-up comedy? The jokes can be really funny. But how much funnier are they with the gestures and the body language of the comedian? How about a great singer? How much better are they with physiology? Michael Jackson and Elvis Presley are arguably two of the best entertainers of all time. My point here, is the voice is not the most powerful form of influence, but the words we utter should have an impact.

I'm going to line up five features to show you how to stack benefits. Let's say the features are for pest control so this product controls pests in and around your home and keeps them away. *Okay, here we go!*

FEATURES

Non-Toxic

Used As A Perimeter

Long-Lasting Formula

Money-Back Guarantee

Certified Installation

Our first feature is that pest control is non-toxic (**Feature**). This means there is no danger of making pets or humans sick. It has a patented technology that does not leave a dangerous residue. So in the event, you decide to go ahead with us (**Embedded Command**), you'll know that you and your pets are safe, giving you a feeling of peace (**Benefits And Feeling**). Not only that (**Benefit Stacker**), we also apply our product to the perimeter so it doesn't go in your home (**Feature**). The benefit here is that we can stop the pests before they get in, so in the event (**Guard Down**) you go ahead with this, here's what you will notice (**Embedded Commands With Future Pace Suggestion**) that you can sleep soundly never wondering if something is crawling around while you sleep. You will know that you and your family are safe and pest-free (**Future Pace**).

In addition to all of that (**Benefit Stacker**), we use a long- lasting formula (**Feature**). The benefit here is that we only have to apply it once a year, typically just before mating season. This ensures that we start to attack before they're even born. We also do this automatically every year, so you don't have to think about it. You'll be confident that you and your family are free from pests, feeling clean and safe (**Benefit And Feeling**). If that's not enough, we also give you (**Benefit Stacker**) a money-back guarantee (**Feature**). Our philosophy is simple - if our product doesn't work, you won't remain a customer.

Once you say, *"Yes"* and *"Go Ahead With Us"* (**Embedded Command**), we want you to be part of the family forever. In the case that we have underperformed, and you still kept on getting pests, your money back is guaranteed. This puts all the risk on us, giving you peace of mind and leaving you feeling satisfied with your choice (**Benefit And Feeling With Future Pace**).

Last but not least, we will even provide you with (**Benefit Stacker**) certified installation from a certified installer (**Feature**). This is very important because the product is only as good as the installation. If done right, it works 100%. So, the nice thing here is we are certified, which means you're safe, no bugs, a bug-free environment where you can sleep comfortably (**Once Again Benefit And Feeling**).

Honestly, I've never sold pest control, but that sounds pretty damn good if I do say so myself. Once you know the formula, you can adapt it to any product, any service, just like that.

ACTION STEP

Study these feature sets I just provided you here and then apply them to your own. This will make a huge difference in your conversions when it is done like this.

Eliminate Shoppers Using Contrast

One of the reasons people shop is because you, the rep, haven't given them anything to compare to. You want to use comparisons to eliminate shoppers, be proactive instead of waiting for it to come up. I'll run you through the last feature set example of pest control, I'll use each one of them and I'll show you how I would use contrast to begin the process of getting them off of shopping in a proactive way.

Feature Number One

Non-toxic. The product we would use here folks is non-toxic. Only 1% of the companies in the business even offer a non- toxic product. With our product, you know you're safe. Does this seem good, or *Great*?

Feature Number Two

Used as a perimeter. You see most pest-control companies, Mr. and Mrs. Smith, do interior chemicals to deal with pests. This is one of the things that makes us very different. How does this feel for you?

Feature Number Three

Long-lasting formula. Mr. and Mrs. Customer, we use a long- lasting formula, unlike the cheaper companies or those, "Here today, gone tomorrow companies trying to save a buck at your expense" type of companies. Does this make sense?

Feature Number Four

Money-back guarantee. Mr. and Mrs. Customer, we've been around for 17 years so we stand behind our money-back guarantee unlike so many of these unproven companies who will be in the game today and out of the game tomorrow leaving you, the customer, hanging. How does this make you feel?

Feature Number Five

Certified installation. Mr. and Mrs. Customer, all too often people are using unskilled labor to do this type of work just to save money. But we live on referrals. It's the lifeblood of our business. That's why we took the time to certify our installers no matter how costly it is. Does this make sense?

I'm using features to bring them to the conclusion that most pest control companies that are cheaper companies are here today and gone tomorrow. I want them to understand that my company is part of the top 1% for service and reliability. What I'm doing here is creating contrast. Also notice that I'm doing it generically. I'm not mentioning any names, but I'm creating some scenarios to get in their head a little bit. Make them think twice and realize that I'm the best choice. By the way, I can even take these feature sets that I've just given to you and put these on steroids by adding even more embedded commands and future pacing. Having them conclude that my product, my company and I are the only solutions. Provided I have a great rapport and that my intention is in the right place, we can deliver and provide all that's in place. You're going to win the business!

The Value Equation & Value Equation Questions (VEQ)

I don't believe that you will find this specific tactic anywhere. Most of these have been put together and are very unique. This is a stylistic thing from a guy named Mark, who is a very technical salesperson, obsessed with influence and persuasion provided there is a healthy view of selling at the base or the foundation.

I'm going to talk to you about what I call a "**Value Equation.**" The reasons why people don't buy is because there's not enough contrast in it. They can't see the value of what you're offering. What does this value equation do? It uses contrast and poses a question to direct their minds in a certain direction. We will use the pest control example. Again, I've never sold pest control in my life; this is just to show you how things are done. I've never even consulted with a company that does pest control so I'm creating these examples as I'm writing this book on the fly. Once you know what you're doing and you understand the patterns, you will be able to do the same thing and apply it to your business. So, here we go!

I'm going back to the feature set that we've been working with, so Feature Number One is it's non-toxic.

> *"So, Mr. Customer, let me ask you a question. My program is non-toxic. If this were to prevent some* sort of poisonous injury and my system cost $1000 more than the nearest toxic competitor, would it be worth more or less than that?"

Most people are going to say more than, based on the value equation. I would finish it by saying;

> *"I've got great news for you! In some cases, our program costs even less!"*

See what I did here? I used contrast. But more importantly, I allowed them to determine the value by merely asking the question and creating the scenario, and then I let them answer. Let me give you another example.

Let's go to the Feature Set Number Two, used on the perimeter.

> *"So, Mr./Mrs. Customer, my program uses pest control on the perimeter if this program kept the pest out of your house, but my system is $1000 more than the nearest competitor's program that doesn't work, would that be worth less than or more than $1000?"*

The customer replies "*More Than*". Then I will say,

> *"I've got great news for you! It's not going to be an additional thousand dollars!"*

You see, we're setting up the contrast or scenarios to create and build value so that they will lean towards us versus another company.

A key distinction here. Notice that there's an implication in almost everything I do; it is with my company, my product, and me. You will get pleasure with me, and pain without me.

This implication runs through my entire selling style and I'm telling you, what if you get what I just said, and you can apply it to your product, company, or service. You might just close at 100% because it is that powerful.

Let me give you one more value equation using **Feature Set Number Three**, long-lasting formula.

> *"Mr./Mrs. Customer, using my long-lasting formula means we are doing it right the first time, unlike other companies. I will be charging an additional thousand dollars, would it be worth less than, or more than the thousand dollars to guarantee that these pests do not invade your home the first time we do it?"*

The customer says, *"Yes!"* So, I replied,

> *"I've got great news for you! It's not going to be another thousand dollars but $2000! No, I'm just joking! It's going to be priced right where everybody else is. The only difference is you have way more benefits if you choose to go ahead with me and my company."*

Friends, out of all the chapters, I'm giving you the most here, in this chapter. You should study and practice this, because there's a lot here. It's a little challenging getting it all into a book and frankly, I just can't, otherwise, I would lose your attention. My goal here is to give you as much as I can and at the same time I want you to realize the difference between a book and coaching, particularly with these results. It's the difference between *"Do It Yourself"* or *"Do It With Your Coach."*

If you do it with me, we can assume that you are done with the book so it's only a matter of practicing, drilling, and rehearsing your craft so you get so good at it, you're printing money. This Happens. It's how people like me go from car salesman to millionaire. And the same could happen for you if you're willing to put in the work! See you in the next chapter.

Action Step

Do the ***Action Steps*** already given.

CHAPTER 9

Get Paid to Persuade, The Anatomy of a High Performing Offer & Close

"Words Have Power"

~ Myra Grant

Notes & Ideas

CHAPTER 9

Get Paid to Persuade, The Anatomy of a High Performing Offer & Close

Back in my early alarm days we used to have this thing called a one-day sale and I was taught to tell this *"Time versus money story"* to create urgency to close a deal. I never believed it, nor did I ever believe in it. I can remember one day being in a demo with my mentor and he slid the price and used the one-day offer. The customer's reply was, *"Do I have to do it today? Can't I have some time to think about it?"* and he told them, *"Well, if you want to get those savings you will have to do it today."* I could just remember their body language and I do remember the way I felt, and it was tense. Mike was a bit high pressure in those days, he didn't really care too much what other people felt like he just saw himself as a closer and he was going to close a deal.

Fortunately, his process did evolve where today he operates from a win-win framework. We're all learning. It was from experiences like that which caused me to innovate this entire closing process. So, what you're about to discover comes from my own experience and it comes from observing other people closely in other industries.

Basically, I'm taking the best of what I've discovered that works, that is honest and ethical, and fits into the framework of positive intention, and a healthy view of selling. It's all been put together for you here to assist you In the ultimate sell without selling, ***No Close, Close***; this is where the title of this book came from.

Prior to showing you the framework of the offer itself and how to slide the price I'm going to do this backwards, I'm going to show you the, **"Four Steps To Gold"** process. The Four Steps To Gold is essentially a close without closing framework. Please know the best way to close is to discover people's problems and solve them through questions. But remember, some people still require some massaging to get to Yes. This framework was developed out of my discomfort for the way my mentor closed deals. Stylistically it just wasn't a good fit for me, so I had to create my own, so if you're ready here we go.

Four Steps To Gold

When you move into the close after you have presented your offer and done your price presentation known as *"sliding the price,"* people will sometimes object. It's important that you train yourself in how to deal with people when they object and that's what the four steps to gold is; it gives you a path to run on. If you follow these four steps, I can tell you with absolute certainty your closing ratio is going up, your stress is coming down, and you will make it easier for people to buy as well. *Here we go.*

Step One, Agreement

The interesting thing about agreement is that this will not only work in a close, it will also work anytime anyone is objecting to you for any reason. This is the ultimate in what some people have coined my style as, *Guard*

Down Selling. The reason they call it my style is because when you look at my style it's all about keeping the customers guard down; reducing sales resistance instead of creating resistance. I teach you how to release the resistance and use embedded commands, reframing and future pacing, because I have discovered it works and it produces results. Is that good, or what? All that said, it's built on solving people's problems with the correct intent and healthy view of selling.

What you might want to do in your industry is to categorize the most common objections you get. Originally I came out of the Alarm Systems business. Today, I'm in solar, so those objections are a little different, but back in the alarm business there were really only five objections: Think about it, shop around, no one-day decision, third-party, contract concern and maybe even a sixth, can't afford it.

Let me show you how Step One, Agreement would work with a few of these.

Think about it, when a Customer replies,

> *"I need to think about it,"*

your reply should only be to agree with them, so the goal is to become an expert at agreement. When you do, you will be assisting your customer in lowering their guard. Here's how you agree,

> *"Mr./Mrs. customer I understand, and I want you to know it's no issue. In fact, if you're not comfortable, I'm not comfortable. In all reality I won't even let you go ahead with it (**Embedded Command**) unless you're completely comfortable."*

Shop around. When the customer replies,

> *"It sounds good, but I think we're going to shop around,"*

Again your reply should be to agree with them.

> *"Now, Mr./Mrs. customer if you're not comfortable, I'm not comfortable, and the only way I'll even let you say yes and go ahead (**Embedded Command**) would be if you were completely comfortable. I'm just not that type of guy."*

I'll do one more for you here just to bring the point home.

Third-party. When the customer replies,

> *"I've got a check with my uncle Harry I want to see what he has to say,"*

Again, your reply should always be to agree with that.

> *"No issue Mr./Mrs. customer. If for any reason you're not entirely certain that this makes incredible sense for you to go ahead with this (**Embedded Command**) I'm not comfortable. The only way I would even let you go ahead (**Embedded Command**) would be if you had total peace about it."*

So, there you have it. Agree with your customer, always agree, always agree, always agree. Keep their guard down.

Step Two, Remove The Words but, or however

This is a transition to step three, where we'll learn to handle the concern, but removing key words is a bridge to get there. If we agree with a customer and then we say, *"but"* or *"however,"* we're basically negating the agreement. We do not want to discredit the agreement. What we have to do is use other words to transition into step three which is handling the concern, does this make sense? Yes? Great! Also, when becoming an agreeable person it will transfer to the customer and you will gain more agreement, this is powerful.

Here are some transition words to help you move from agreement into step three handling the concern.

Transition Words.

- One thing you might want to consider is...
- I've dealt with many people with a similar concern, here's what we've discovered...
- Through years of experience, I've noticed that this comes down to one of three things...
- No need to sweat these right now because you have to see how it all comes together. As you do, I know you will love this process.

Step Three, Handle The Concern

The first objection was to think about it, so the reply would sound something like this,

> *"Through years of experience, I've noticed that this typically comes down to one of three things. Number one - Do you feel like you need the product? And earlier we discussed your need for the product, and you said, 'Yes, that makes sense.' Do you still feel the same way?"*

NOTE: If *Yes*, go to the next step, if No, you might need to address the need (you didn't solve the problem in their mind). Assuming *Yes*:

> *Excellent! I agree that you really do need this. Secondly I had asked you If you were excited about this product and the solution and how this could*

stop your pain in its tracks and you had said, 'Yes,' do you still feel the same way?"

NOTE: If No, there's probably something else lingering. If Yes, excellent, reframe the money and here's how.

"Mr./Mrs. customer I know that the investment here may seem like a little more than you planned for. That said, do you realize that this is only X dollars per week (reduce it). My question is, if all this did was (if all statements - more on this later) stop the pain one time over the next one year three years, five years, 10 years would it be worth every bit of that or would it have been worth more?

Customer: *"Well, more!"*

You have to learn how to break money down, reduce to the ridiculous and how to reframe. When you reframe, you shift from the money to the value and then we are ready to move to step four, which will be prompt action.

Step Four, Prompt Action

This is a step that salespeople often forget because they struggle with the fear of rejection. They feel the tension in the customer, and they don't want to get rejected. So often sales people just avoid doing this. In order for you to master this game you must learn to prompt action. Notice I don't practice *Assumptive Selling*, especially in the early part of the demo.

Nowhere have you heard me speak of *Assumptive Selling*. That's because I'm not a practitioner of it and frankly I don't care for it. I'm into earning the right to sell based on positive intent, a healthy view of selling by understanding people's needs and desires. If you fulfill the needs and desires and do it in a win-win way by adding tons of value that allows you to express yourself through a product you love; that is my formula.

KEY POINT: Now we're in the close, this is all about increasing your level of urgency. Finding the urgency within yourself and within your offer and transferring that to your customer without being manipulative while still being brutally honest. Let me show you how to prompt action.

You've agreed with the customer, you transitioned beautifully without using the words, *"but"* or *"however,"* and you have handled the concerns likely through reframing, now it's time to prompt action.

Here's an example from Solar,

> *"Mr. and Mrs. customer you can wait, and I can wait, but that CEO of the electric company never waits. He or she is sitting on the sidelines waiting to raise your rates as we speak, not to mention their $20 million earnings, so what do you say we take the bull by the horns and never be at their mercy again? Let's get this over with once and for all, fair enough?"*

Here's an example from my Alarm Business.

> *"Mr. and Mrs. Smith you can wait, and I can wait, but bad guys never wait. Based on the existing holes in your current security what do you say we close the barn door before the horse gets out, fair enough?"*

Here's an example for the insurance industry.

> *"Mr. and Mrs. Smith you can wait, and I can wait, unfortunately untimely death never waits, it shows up like a thief in the night. Let's take the bull by the horns and get you this desperately needed protection once and for all, fair enough?"*

ACTION REQUIRED

Because we have limited time in a book, I'm going to make you all a special offer where you can access ***"Mark's Greatest Closing Hits,"*** a special free video training series designed to take this a little deeper. Access it now by going to **www.MarkTosoni.com/closinghits**

THE OFFER

NOW I'm going to show you the framework of the offer and how to slide the price. This is a science in and of itself and if you're not doing this scientifically, I can guarantee you you're losing tons of leverage, contribution, and money. With just a little adjustment in this part of your demo could take you from average, to good, to great.

Slide the price sheet. For starters, in order for this to be scientific and replicable you've got to create and slide the price sheet. I will give you the following elements that the sheet should include. And I'll show you an example of a sheet, a template, that you can merely fill-in. Every industry is different, so you've got to play around with this to make it work for you in your business or industry.

Back in the day I had a ***"Total Slide The Price Sheet"*** for my alarm business sales team, which is in my book, Alarm Sales Mastery. Today I am in solar, and solar is a return on investment (ROI) sale. There are elements of this template that will work very well there as well. So, you've got to adapt this to your offering.

NOTE: This comes from years of experience as well as looking outside of the industry into coaching and consulting, how to do webinars and the mechanics of that and platform selling. As I said before I love crossing industrics and learning from others because there's so many best practices that can be applied to different businesses.

What you will see below is an innovation from various industries and what works and produces results within them. Here's what I know for sure, if all you did was implement this template, your conversions are going up. You will also have feedback on your full demos, what took place, what went right, what went wrong, that feedback is priceless whether you are out selling or building sales teams. So here we go,

Product / Service Offer Template
The Feature Summary Bonuses, If Applicable
Slide The Price Total Value
"If All" Statements
Actual Price
Testimonials/Closes
Prompt Action/Call To Action (CTA)

The Feature Summary

So here you will actually list out the features of your offer. The important thing here is to understand that your customer doesn't know the terminology and what it really means. Most of what you say, they lose, so it's important to do this during your demo but also to recap it when you're making the offer. I've already explained to you how to speak in benefits and feelings. You would do the exact same thing here when you are recapping your feature set.

Bonuses, If Applicable

If your offer has bonuses you would add them here. It's a good idea to offer bonuses because the bonuses make the offer more valuable. This will raise your compliance level, especially if you have high value bonuses that solve major pain points. This is more common in the coaching and consulting world than it is in the tangible products world such as in-home sales, however it doesn't have to be. In-home homies take a page out of the consultants playbook and add some bonuses to your offer or turn some of your existing offerings into bonuses so they will have higher perceived value, just an FYI.

Slide The Price

Give them the price of the total value, "*Under normal circumstances this is the price.*" But this is not the price you will sell this for. This price is what it is actually worth, and the objective here is to justify this price. If you can't justify it at the higher value you're going to have a hard time getting a "*Yes*" at the actual price.

"If All" Statements

For many years in the alarm business I used to use, *"If You Knew For Sure,"* statements. Then I learned about these statements called, *"If All" Statements.*" They are commonly used by a friend of mine Dave van Hoose, who is a really well-known platform sales person and consultant. The way these work is that you basically ask the question,

> *"If all this did was (fill in the blanks), would it be worth every bit and then some?"*

The idea in the *"If All"* statements is to get them to say "*Yes*" three times. So again,

> *"If all this did was (fill in the blank some more), would it be worth less than or more than (the value price)?" And again, "If all this did was (solve another pain point), is it fair to say it would be worth every bit of what we were originally asking?"*

The idea in the "*If All*" statements is to get the three yes's.

The Actual Price

Now you present the actual price. "Folks, I've got great news for you. Instead of it costing you the original price of X, your actual investment will only be Y. Isn't that discount exciting?"

Testimonials And Closes

Here is a great place to go through three testimonials that have your top three objections. Use trial closes which I also like to call, *"An enthusiastic 'Yes'* set." More on those in a moment.

Prompt action/Call to action (CTA). Here is where you ask for the business. I'm a big believer in prompting; helping them to say, *"Yes."* That's why my favorite words are, *"Say Yes,"* and, *"Go Ahead."*

So these are the elements of the offer, and it will be your homework and action step to compose each of these elements in your offer. The better job you do with it, the better the results you produce. Your conversions will be taken to the bank, it's all proven and will work for you as well as it has for so many others.

Trial Closes

Who's ready to talk about trial closes? How many of you would be excited to learn the skill of trial closing so you could make you a ton of money? What if trial closes we're such a powerful tool that they brought new choices to your life, would that be exciting? What if they brought the choice of the car you like to drive or the home you'd like to live in or the vacations you've been dreaming about taking, would it be exciting to know how to do this?

What you've just read we're a series of trial closes. Essentially a trial close should be used throughout your entire demonstration. I like to call these an *"Enthusiastic 'Yes' Set,"* because you're enthusiastically getting the prospect into, "*Yes*" mode, building momentum towards the close. The invitation is for you to learn to ask questions enthusiastically that lead people to "*Yes.*" This creates a momentum towards the close so when you get to the close the momentum has already been built.

What so many do is they don't get any momentum, and then they try to close a deal, and it's like lifting boulders. I know these pages will make those hurdles a little easier to jump over. Remember to build trial close questions that lead to, *"Yes"* enthusiastically throughout your demonstration. You cannot do too many of these.

to learn more trial closes go to
www.MarkTosoni.com/trialclose

Thank you for being part of this amazing journey with me. I know you've learned a lot. The key is to take what you've learned and add it to your arsenal and take action on it. You can go to any chapter and put that to work in your demonstration immediately and you will see results. If you want to see great results study this book and these plays, if you desire mega-results come coach with me. I cordially invite you.

I can promise you that your investment in time and money will be the best investment you've made in your life, and will pay you back massive dividends, not only in your business life in the form of money, but on an internal level in the form of spiritual wisdom which translates to you becoming wealthy.

That would be my wish and prayer for you as I would never want to see anybody struggle as I had to in my early days. My intention and prayer is that this work will help to eliminate, or at least alleviate your struggle and make your path a little easier than mine has been. If you receive that, say, "*Yes!*" God bless and Godspeed, chat with you real soon.

Action Step

Practice *The Four Steps To Gold.*

CHAPTER 10

Conclusion /Summary

"For the sales driven entrepreneur who has chosen wealth obstacle immunity is mandatory."

~ Mark Tosoni

Notes & Ideas

CHAPTER 10

Conclusion/Summary

The *Game Of Selling* is changing, and will continue to change as life continues to get more complex. Because of COVID-19, more salespeople are doing presentations online and wearing masks. You must be able to adapt and adapt quickly. That said, the fundamentals of the game don't change all that much. This book is an invitation to master some fundamentals and level up your skills so no matter what changes we face as a nation and in sales as an occupation, you will be the best prepared of your peers and competitors.

This book is a book of skills and distinctions that will not only prepare you for what you are dealing with but help you gain the edge and master the game of selling. Interestingly enough, it all begins with mindset. This book begins with mindset as much of my coaching, some 80%, deals with what's going on inside of you. I've observed through my coaching that this is what moves the needle and gets salespeople paid. Still, a master SKILL SET is also required for the strategies in this book.

From there we went into the purpose of *Your Sales Career*. In my own point of view, I believe this is one of the single best distinctions of this book because everything you do stems from your perception of why you are doing it. Here I explained an emphasis on serving and solving other people's problems throughout your sales process with your product or service offering.

If that wasn't strong enough, we then went onto a **Healthy View Of Selling** which is a philosophy. It's very clear that other people pick up on your intentions. This positions you as a person who is there at the sales appointment to serve, and to solve their problems first and foremost, even though the overarching purpose of your career is to become financially free. When you marry chapters one through three, you truly have an unfair advantage in the sales game and will win over lots of business that is there for the taking.

The book quickly became tactical in chapter four with some **Fundamental Rapport Building Skills**. Built on chapters two and three, it becomes even more powerful with a combination of results producing ingredients that will enhance the results of the amateur all the way up to the expert. I introduced you to some new school ideas with **ways of being**. This has been a priceless distinction for me in my never-ending quest to understand and communicate with people through their lens. This will do the exact same for you, providing certainty for your career along with recognition, variety and a sense of connection to others.

As far as tactics are concerned, Chapter Five is the Best Of The Best of what I've discovered and it works especially well when layered on to what was discovered in chapters one through three. These are the *Mixed Martial Arts Of Selling Skills Guaranteed To Result In Victory After Victory.* The customer experiences victory because you will be solving their problems en masse. I recommend diving in deeply to this section, and of course if you coach with me in the future I will definitely do a deep dive around these master skills.

I recently taught the contents of Chapter Five to my own sales team and doubled the sales the very next week to more than $3 million. ***Hot Buttons*** are that powerful! This process builds confidence and clarity for the salesperson and customer. Nothing could be more powerful. Objections occur when there is uncertainty in the communication. This process solves that forever. It's tested in multiple industries and will produce for you in any interactive presentation.

In Chapter Seven, I show you a tactic that will lead you to more sales than you can imagine. My own sales team uses this daily in our presentations right before we give them the breakdown of the investment. It's an enhancement to the sales process that is much needed especially in commission sales, car sales and in-home financial services. You'd be really making your life more difficult by not adding this time-tested tactical weapon.

And of course, in Chapter Eight, I show you a new way to handle objections and concerns which, regardless of sales style, will occur. To think they won't occur (as some teach), is like getting into a fight and expecting not to get hit; even the masters get hit, you must be prepared. This chapter prepares you not only for objections, but all sales resistance. You will handle it like a pro, and as a result you will make a lot more money.

Finally, in Chapter Nine, you were introduced to more tactics to strengthen your offer and buying desire. All of these tactics in this chapter will make the process flow with more ease and less stress for you and your customer. Remember, when in a selling situation, fear can come up on both sides, diffuse it on your side with master positioning and skill.

I know with complete certainty you can go to any chapter on any day and do sales meetings for yourself if needed or for a large group. The content of this work will remain timeless for years to come. I'm inviting you to make the investment for real by embodying what you've discovered through these pages. When you will have made the world a better place, you will have made a massive contribution to the game of selling. Enhance the lives of your prospects who are now customers and move yourself towards your ultimate purpose of complete financial freedom. *I will see you in coaching really soon!*

Thank you for reading my book!

Mark Tosoni

Books by Mark Tosoni

Money Attraction Secrets

Get Coached, Get Rich

Six Figure Commission Sales Secrets

Say Yes To Solar

Alarm Sales Mastery

Quotes For An Exceptional Life

Sell Like Crazy Without Going Insane

Fast Strategies For Maximum Influence

The Art and Science of Success

The Secret To Winning Big (featured writer)

The Closers Part 5, Mark Tosoni & Ben Gay

Made in United States
Orlando, FL
04 November 2026

90201210R00085